People and Places

SOCIAL SCIENCE PUPIL BOOK

Department of Education
Papua New Guinea

First Published 1988
Reprinted 1990, 1993, 1994, 1995, 1996 (twice), 1997, 1998, 1999 (three times), 2000 (twice), 2002, 2008, 2013(D)

ISBN 9980 58209 X
ISBN 978 9980 58209 6
National Library of Papua New Guinea

Cover photograph by courtesy of the University of Papua New Guinea and Jose Reis

Written by Peter Bridger
Designed by Steve Randles
Illustrated by Annie Irish and Chris Johnston
Typeset by Abb Typesetting Pty Ltd. Collingwood, Victoria, Australia
Printed in Australia by Ligare Pty Ltd
Published by Department of Education, Papua New Guinea
Prepared by Oxford University Press
253 Normanby Road, South Melbourne, Australia

Acknowledgements

The Papua New Guinea Department of Education acknowledges the contribution of many individuals at the Curriculum Unit, the University of Papua New Guinea, the National Museum, and on the Social Science Syllabus Advisory Committee to the trialling and review of the book. The participation of the teachers and students at the trial schools — Kilakila, Badihagwa, Laloki, Gerehu, and Tusbab — is greatly appreciated.

The authors and publishers wish to thank copyright holders for supplying, and granting permission to reproduce the following photographs and maps:

Acme News Pictures Inc., p. 2 (lower); Associated Press Ltd, p. 6 (upper right); Australian Overseas Information Service, pp. 7 (lower), 36 (left); CSIRO, p. 3 (lower centre); Embassy of Brazil, Canberra, p. 3 (lower right); Fox Photos, London, p. 4 (right); Hsinhua News Agency, p. 2 (third from top); J.W. Lindt, courtesy of the PNG Department of Information and Extension Services, pp. 36 (right), 37 (left); Mitchell Library, p. 37 (upper right); National Film Board of Canada, p. 3 (upper centre); National Mapping, p. 38 (upper); Post Courier, p. 6 (left); Press Association Photos, p. 33; Reuters News Picture Library, p. 2 (upper); Ronél Ruffles, p. 3 (upper right); D. Simpson, p. 17 (left); Timothy G. Wright, p. 5 (right).

Secretary's Message

The topic **People and Places** is the third term's work in the Grade Eight Provincial High School Social Science Course. It is the second of four topics which develop the theme of **Living Together** through Grades Seven to Ten.

The book is the core learning material for the topic. A supporting set of teaching notes is available. The teaching notes advise the teachers on how to make the best use of the pupil's book.

The material in the book integrates the presentation of information, the development of ideas, reinforcement and application of Social Science skills and the fostering of attitudes.

Three types of activities are at the end of each section. There are *Exercises* to ensure comprehension of the material; there are *Things to do* and *Things to discuss*. The activities combine work on sections of the book with direct investigations both inside and outside school.

J.E. Tetaga
Secretary for Education

This book is one of the items of instructional material produced for Provincial High Schools in Papua New Guinea as part of the Education III Textbook Sub-Project.

Contents

1. Communities

In this book we will learn about **people** and the **places** where they live.

Human beings have always lived in groups. Wherever people live together they form communities. Some communities are very small; others are very big.

A community is not just a place in the environment. It is a place where people meet and **interact** with each other. People have **needs,** things they must have in order to survive, and they have **wants**, things they would like which make life easier. People meet their needs and satisfy their wants through activities with other people. Each person who belongs to a community has an important part to play in it.

People's Needs and Wants

Every person has needs and wants. It is often very difficult to get everything you need or want by yourself. People have found that, by living together, they can co-operate with each other to satisfy their needs and wants.

This diagram below illustrates some of the needs and wants of people living in a community. Can you think of any other needs or wants? Which of the things shown are essential for people to live?

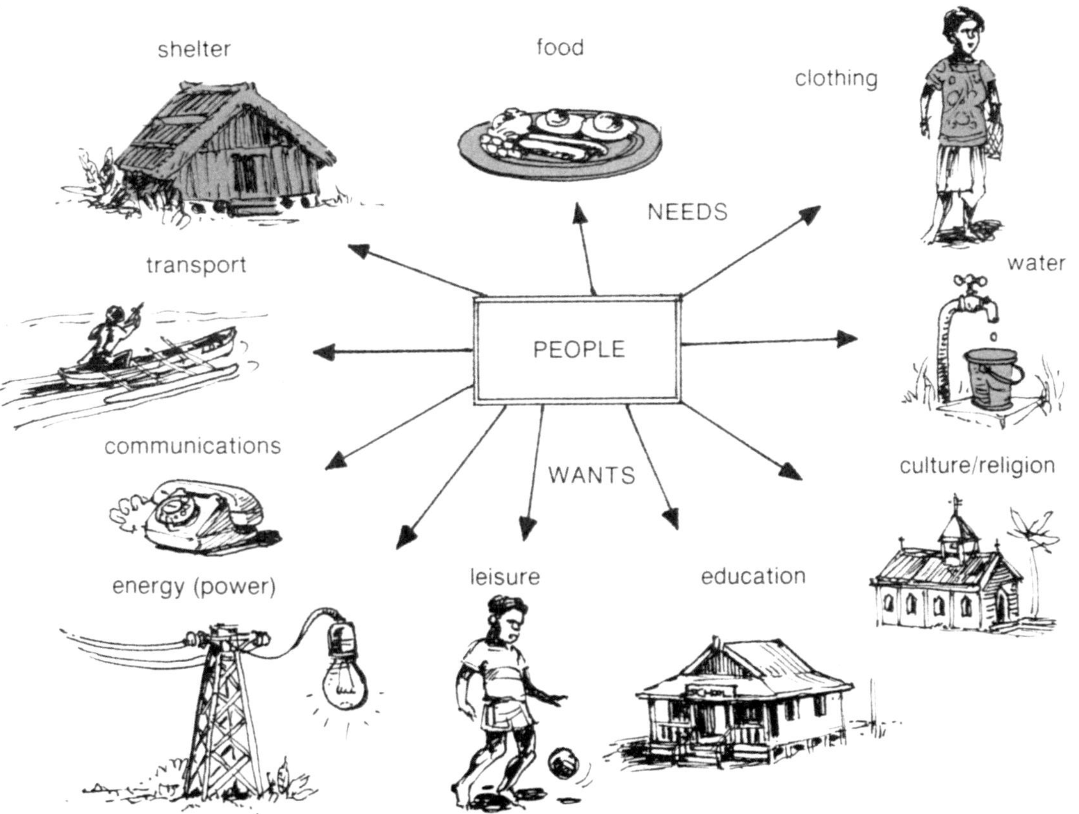

People in a community interact with each other. Each person makes something, or performs a service, that other people need or want. All people have a responsibility to look after and educate the children and to care for the older people who can no longer do things.

People become specialised at doing one particular thing. This is called their role. In this way the community supplies most of its needs and wants.

People live in places that have a particular advantage to them. They depend on the environment and the things it provides. The things in the environment that people use are called resources.

Communities are organised to make the best use of their resources. Different communities are organised in different ways; for example, some are organised according to their **religion**, others are organised according to different political beliefs.

Environment

There are many different climates in the world. The climate of a place determines the type of vegetation that grows there, the crops that people grow, the style of house that they build, and people's activities throughout the year. The map opposite shows the main types of climate in the world. The communities we will study in this book are shown in some of the photographs.

Nomadic herders in Lapland

Rural farming in England

Threshing the corn in Tibet

Nomadic tribes in North-East Africa

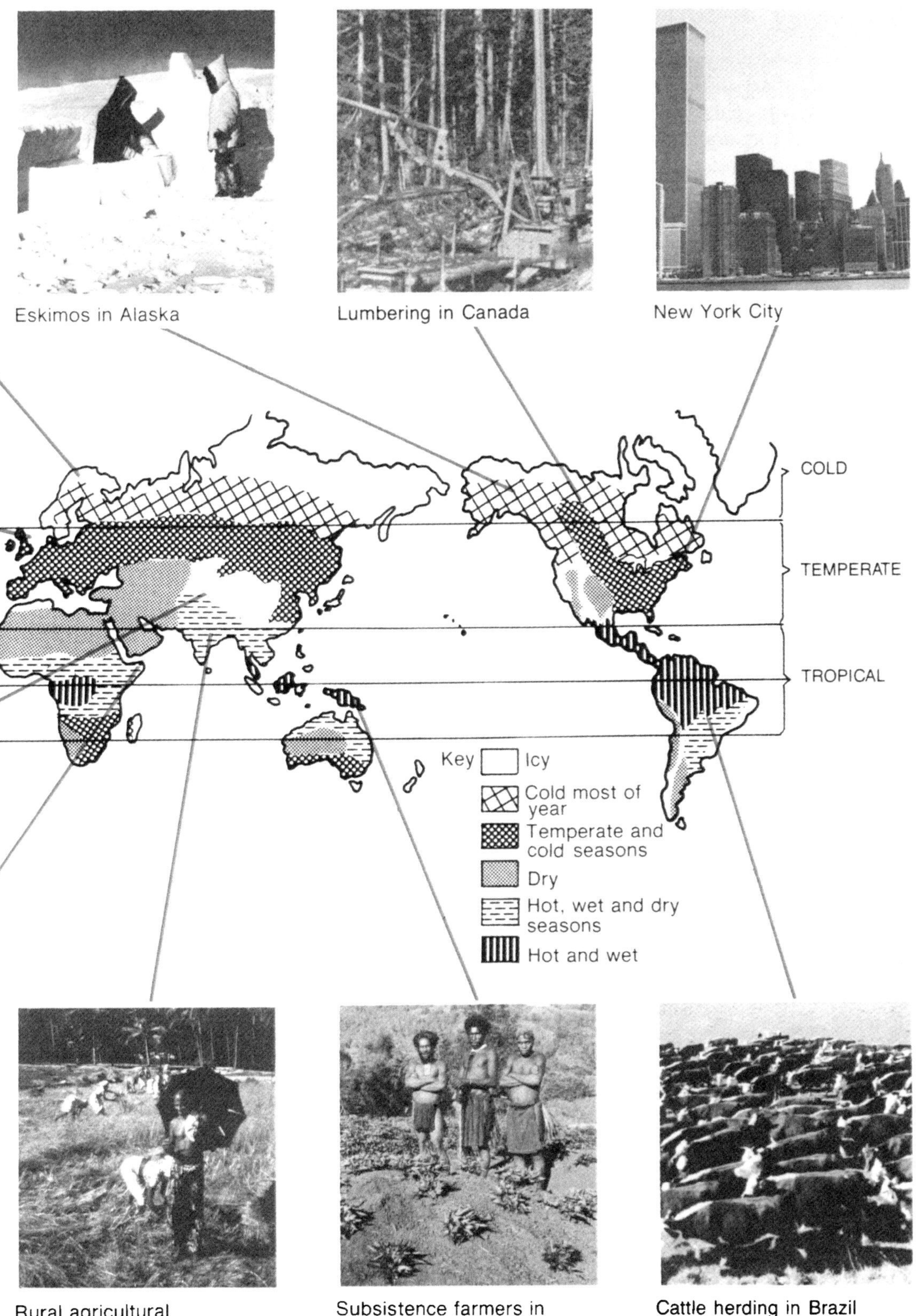

Eskimos in Alaska

Lumbering in Canada

New York City

Rural agricultural community in India

Subsistence farmers in Papua New Guinea

Cattle herding in Brazil

Resources

People choose to live where they can best satisfy their needs for shelter, food and water. This depends on the resources of the environment they live in. The climate and vegetation of an area often determines the type of houses people build.

The main resource of most communities is water. Many communities are located close to a supply of water. All people **need** water to drink. Water is also used for cooking, washing and for watering gardens. Many communities in Papua New Guinea are located close to a stream or river.

Rivers are important resources for communities. However, a river can be a barrier for people who wish to travel on land. People can cross rivers only where they are shallow and can be forded, or where they are narrow enough to build a bridge across. People travel to places where the rivers can be crossed easily. Communities have developed in such places. London, the capital city of England, started in this way. It is on a part of the river that can be bridged. This place is also very close to the sea. It has been an important crossing point for over 2000 years and has become an important trading centre.

Aerial view of London showing the River Thames and its bridges.

Where People Live

Near rivers

The village in the photograph is on the banks of the Sepik River. The people here use the river for drinking, washing and watering gardens. They also use the river for fishing and to travel from one place to another. Whenever the river floods onto the flat land close to the banks, it leaves behind a layer of rich alluvial soil. This is good for growing crops.

A village on a river bank.

On the coast

The sea is an important resource. Many groups of people live on the coast. They obtain most of their food from the sea. Their houses are usually built close to the shore in order to protect their canoes. They also choose places that are sheltered from strong winds and large waves so that the houses are not destroyed. Large bays and inlets are sheltered and many villages can be found in these places. The Motuan people built their villages in Fairfax Harbour because it is sheltered from the strong south-easterly winds. The white settlers who built Port Moresby chose this place for the same reason. Nowadays Port Moresby is a busy port because even large ships can anchor there in safety.

Port Moresby harbour.

Hilltops

Some communities are located a long way from water. The village in the photograph is located on the top of a ridge. The houses have been built here for two reasons:

1. the ridge is close to the community's food gardens;
2. the village is easy to defend against attack from neighbouring tribes.

The women walk a long way each day to fetch water from the stream in the bottom of the valley.

A village on a hilltop.

Other places

Communications are very important to all communities. Air transport has played a large part in the development of the rural areas of our country. Wau and Bulolo in Morobe Province became important gold-mining centres in the 1920s. Air transport was used to carry most of the heavy mining equipment into the area. Missions and a government station were established to look after the people who came to Wau to live. The gold is not very important today but the airstrip is still used. There is still quite a large township there because it is close to the airstrip, an important link with the rest of Papua New Guinea.

Dredges and aeroplanes at Bulolo.

Organisation

Communities differ in the ways they are organised. People's cultures, religions and values vary from place to place.

All countries have some form of government. In some countries leaders are elected **democratically**. This means that the people choose their leaders by voting for them. The leaders in turn try to help the people who voted for them. The elected leaders form a government that is responsible for managing the affairs of the country. The communities in the country are free to choose the way they live.

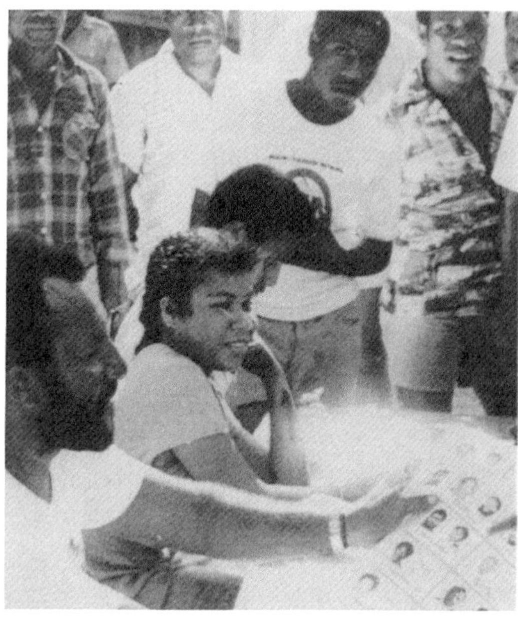

Voting at a polling station during the 1987 general election.

In other countries strong people take power without the people's support. Communities in these countries are not free to choose their way of life and are often told what to do by the government.

Papua New Guinea has an elected government, but, in the villages, elders and family heads still have high status. They often act as community leaders.

There are many countries in the world where religious beliefs control people's lives. Religious leaders have high status in these countries, and direct people's activities. For example, the photograph below shows thousands of Muslims called to prayer by their religious leaders. In Muslim countries this is a daily event.

Muslims at Mecca, their holy city.

Community Activities

People in a community meet often and share skills and ideas with each other. Each person has a part to play (a role) in the life of the community.

This photograph shows people pounding rice to make flour in Malaysia. Children all take turns. In this way they learn a skill that will be important to them later in life.

Pounding rice to remove the husk from the grain.

Learning is a very important activity in all communities. Children must learn all the skills they will need to live a happy life. These young boys are learning how to fish. When they grow up and have a family of their own they will need this skill.

Learning to fish.

In modern communities people work for money. They must be able to read and write and to add up. Some people in the community are good at these things and teach them to the children. Communities build schools for these teachers to work in.

Types of Community

Over half the people in the world live in rural communities. The pie graph shows the proportion of people who live in rural and in urban communities.

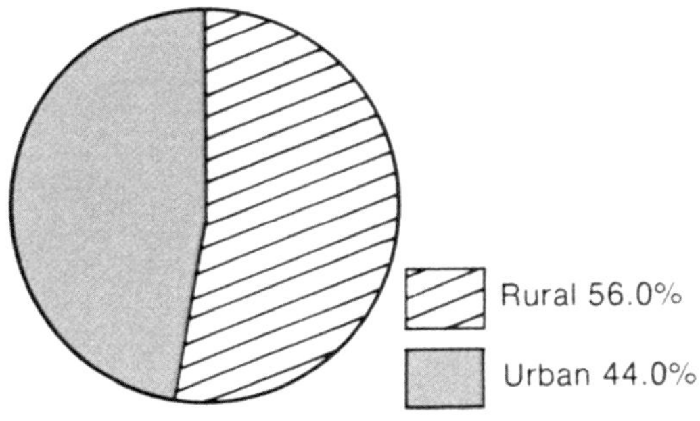

World population — 1985.

People in rural communities are usually involved in growing crops or rearing animals. Some work in the mining, forestry or plantation industries. These are called primary activities. There is very little manufacturing (making things from primary products) in rural areas. The level of technology used is usually low. Services, such as health care, transport and education, are often not well developed.

Urban communities are those in towns and cities. There are many buildings for different purposes and many people work there. Urban centres usually have more resources and better services than rural areas. People's activities are mainly concerned with manufacturing. Making things from primary products is a secondary activity. Many workers also provide services (tertiary activities) for the large number of people there. However, urban communities have problems that are unknown in rural areas.

Urban and rural areas.

In this book we will study some rural communities and some urban communities. We will study a rural community that must survive in a very isolated area, a self-contained community living in a harsh climate, a complex rural community in India, and a rural community that depends on a nearby urban centre for most of its resources. We will also study three very different and separate aspects of communities in Papua New Guinea's largest urban centre, Port Moresby.

In each chapter we will look first at the environment in which the people live. We will then study the people's activities and the way they have organised their communities within this environment.

Summary

A **community** consists of people living in the same area who work together to satisfy their needs and wants.

Communities are not all the same because they have different:

- environments
- resources
- organisations.

Members of a community have particular roles to play.

People become specialised at certain activities, but share their skills and ideas for the benefit of the whole community.

Education is important in all communities.

There are important differences between rural and urban communities.

Urban communities use many buildings for many different purposes.

Activities

Exercise

Look up the meanings of the following words and write a sentence to explain what each one means:

(a) democratic
(b) Muslim
(c) community
(d) status
(e) dictatorship

Give an example of a country where each of these may be found.

Things to discuss

1. Discuss your needs and wants for the following situations:
   (a) living at school
   (b) living in a village
   (c) living in an urban centre.
   What needs are the same for all these places?
   What needs are different?
   How do your wants differ for each place?
2. Compare the organisation of your school with the way your village community is organised. How are the different communities similar or different?

Things to do

1. Copy the following table into your exercise book. For each of the places listed, write down two advantages and one disadvantage of living in each.

PLACE	ADVANTAGES	DISADVANTAGES
Near the sea		
Near rivers		
On the hilltops		

2. Study the photographs and map on pages 2 and 3. Copy the following table into your exercise book. Complete the table for each photograph by writing the name of the continent the community is in, whether the community is urban or rural, and the type of climate found there.

PHOTOGRAPH	URBAN/ RURAL	CONTINENT	CLIMATE
Farming in England			
Herders in Lapland			
Himalayas			
North-East African herders			
Rice in India			
PNG Farmers			
Brazil			
New York City			
Alaska			

3. **(a)** Make a list of the resources available in your village community.
   (b) Make a list of the resources available in your school.
   (c) How do the two lists differ?

4. **(a)** Draw a sketch map and write a paragraph to describe where your home is located.
   (b) Explain why your village was built where it is. What special advantages are there in the environment where you live?

2. Rural Communities: Pataku Island

Pataku is located about 200 kilometres north-west of Manus Island. It is one of the 40 small islands that make up the Ninigo group. There are only about 20 families living on the island, about 150 people in all. Because of their isolation the people are dependent on each other and they co-operate with each other in many activities.

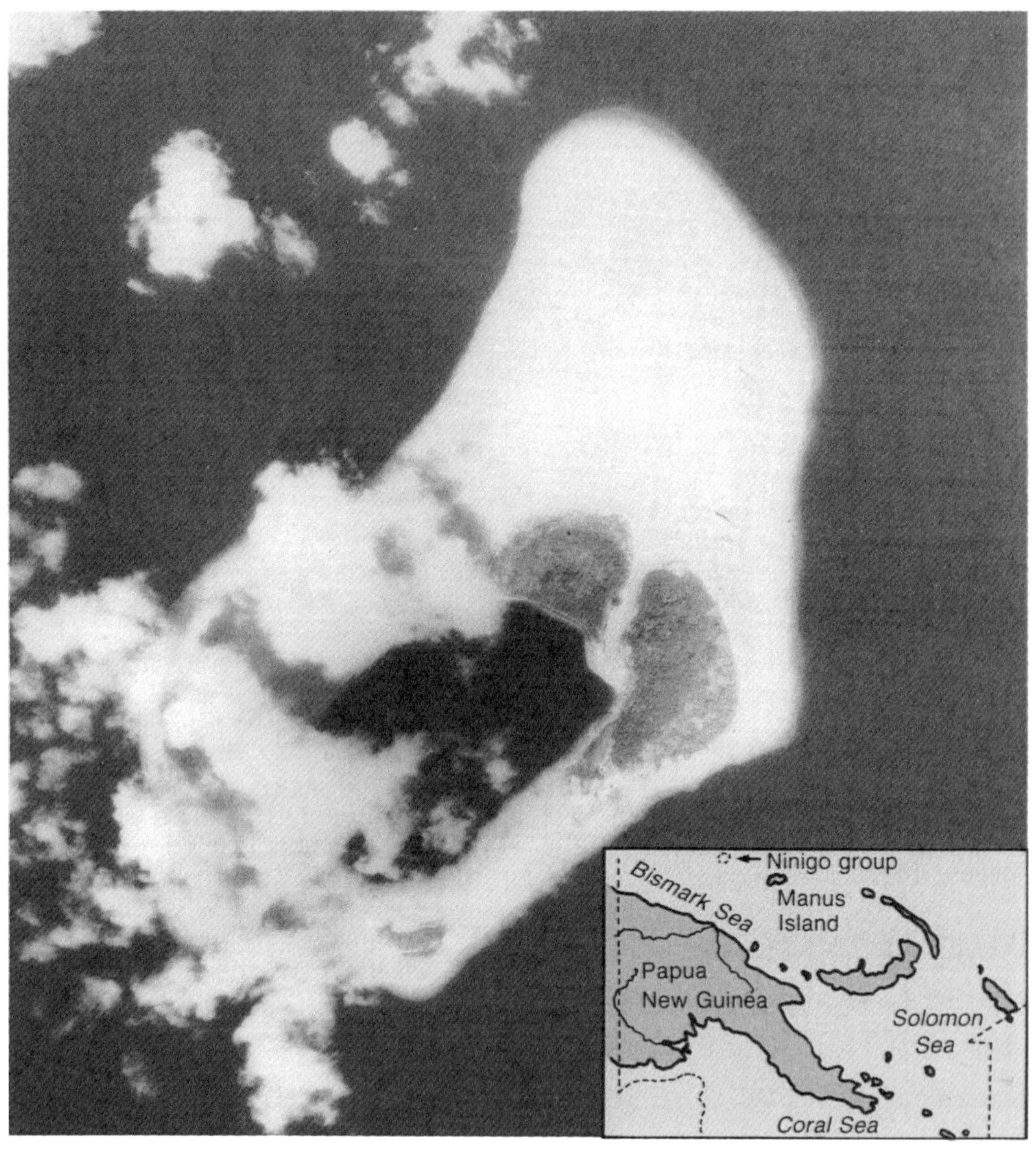

Aerial view of Pataku. Inset map shows the location of Pataku in Papua New Guinea.

Environment

Pataku Island is part of an **atoll.** The island is made out of coral. The soil is very sandy and it is not very fertile.

The climate is hot all the year round, and there are two seasons in the year. From April to September the winds blow from the south-east, the sea is usually calm, and the skies are clear for long periods. From October to March the winds blow from the north-west, the opposite direction. They are quite strong and the sea is rough. Rain and thunderstorms are common in this season.

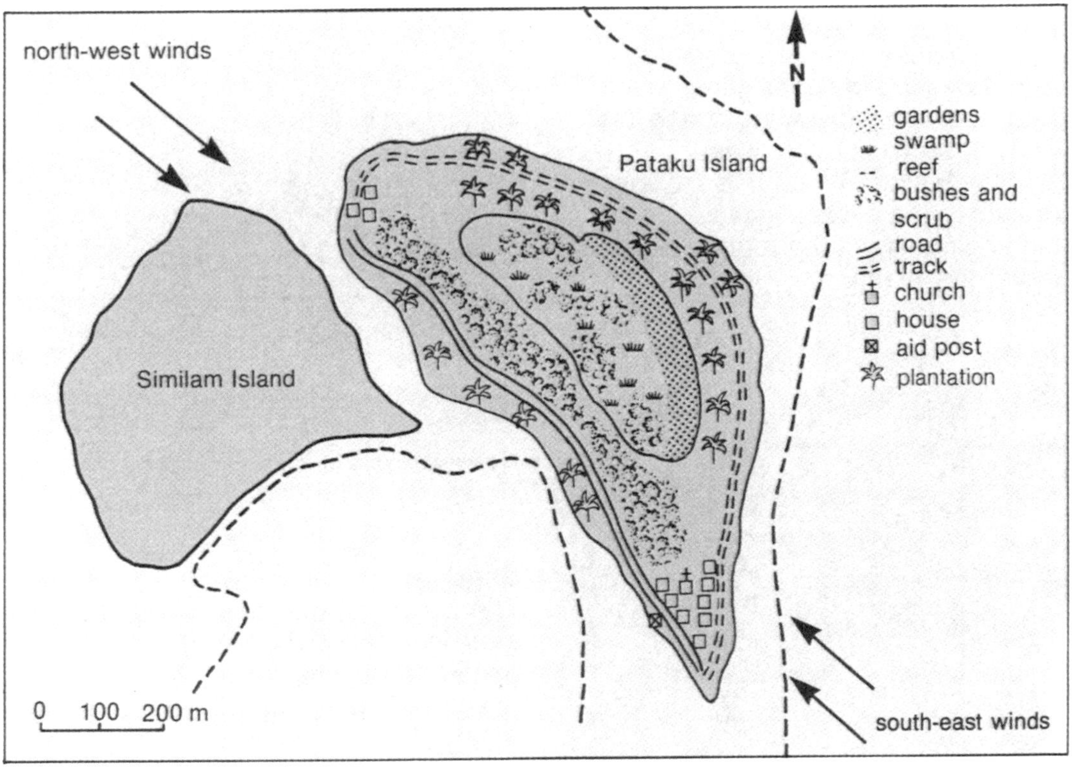

Map of Pataku showing the direction of winds.

Coral is formed by tiny animals called polyps. They make a hard shell and live inside it. Millions of coral polyps live together and, as old ones die, new ones grow on top of them. This is how coral reefs are formed.

An atoll is a circular coral reef growing round a hill or mountain under the water. As more coral grows the reef gets bigger and bigger. Eventually the reef grows so close to the surface of the water that it becomes an island.

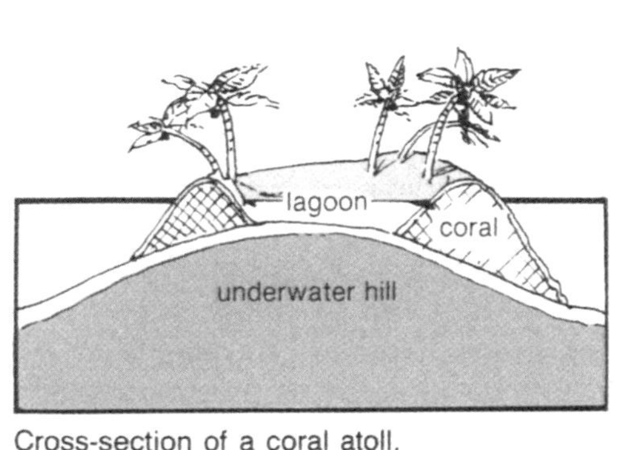

Cross-section of a coral atoll.

Resources

Fishing

The main resources of the islanders come from the sea. They get most of their food from the sea. During the calm season the people use traditional methods of fishing. The *ka'a*, shown in the photograph, is made from twisted-together coconut leaves and all the men must work together to catch fish with it. Modern methods of fishing, such as nets and spear guns, are used by a few individuals during the windy season, but only when conditions allow. When it is too rough for fishing the people harvest clams and shellfish from the reef at the north end of the island.

Traditional fishing — the *Ka'a* showing the coconut leaves twisted together.

Gardening

Very little gardening is done because the soil is sandy and very poor. Some people grow a little sweet potato (*kaukau*), Chinese taro, banana and tapioca. Tapioca is the most useful food crop as it can be dried and stored. In the middle of the island *hula*, a giant taro, grows around some swamps. The people do not take all the hula at one time because it takes a long time to grow. They **conserve** their resources by limiting the hula harvest.

Harvesting hula in the inland swamps.

Sharing

The people of the community share all their food. After the fish is brought ashore the women make sure that everyone has enough for the evening meal. The left-over fish are dried and smoked over a fire to preserve them for future use. Turtles are a particular favourite, and whenever one is caught many people gather together to share it.

Houses

The houses on Pataku are mostly built with local materials. Modern materials, such as corrugated iron, have been used, but they are expensive and quickly corrode in the sea air. The roofs and walls are made out of woven-together coconut and sago leaves. There are no big trees on

Pataku, and so the wooden frames of the houses are made from driftwood collected on the beach. Even the canoes are made from logs that have washed up on the shore.

The bush material aid post with woven-leaf walls and roof.

Cash crops

The people now own a coconut plantation that was first started by German colonists many years ago. They make copra and sell it on the mainland. The **cash income** from the copra has improved the standard of living. People can now afford to buy modern utensils and clothes, and food to supplement their traditional diet.

A coconut plantation.

Organisation

Leadership

On Pataku the village elects one person whose job is to organise activities such as cleaning the aid post or maintaining the track that runs from one end of the island to the other (about 40 minutes walk). Often he consults with the village elders about how a particular job should be done. All members of the community take part in the tasks he organises.

The whole Ninigo group now has a community government. One person is elected from Pataku to represent the island's interests. He also acts as the village magistrate, although most of his cases are social problems and not criminal.

Culture and religion

The Catholic church was one of the first outside influences to reach Pataku. The people very quickly became confirmed Catholics and abandoned all their old customs and traditions. Today, none of the children know any of their traditional dances. The people no longer have a national dress.

Isolation

The island is very isolated. This means that it is a long way from most of the government services. The government boat visits only once every three weeks. It brings supplies and mail and carries away the copra to be sold.

It is important to maintain communications in case of an emergency. The nearest hospital is at Lorengau (Lombrum) on Manus Island. The villagers use a "walkie-talkie" (a hand-held radio) to communicate with other islands.

The young children must attend primary school on Laualau Island, about 40 kilometres to the north-east of Pataku. The nearest high school is on Manus Island.

Manus High School.

Business group

To help meet their needs and wants better, the Pataku community joined with other islands in 1974 to form a business group. This group sells the copra and distributes the benefits to all its members. The group has been able to buy its own boat to improve communications with the rest of the country. Some of the money people earn from the copra is put into a general education fund to help pay school fees. Only a few of the educated people have come back to live and help develop the island. However, many of those who have moved to other centres in Papua New Guinea send money and goods back to the island.

Coastal vessel.

Summary

Pataku is an isolated, rural community.

People's activities are determined by the climate:

- fishing season is from April to August
- clam harvesting takes place from October to March.

The resources of the island are:

- the fish in the area
- shellfish on the reef
- hula, and a few other food plants
- a coconut plantation.

Sharing is an important part of life.

Isolation has resulted in slow development of the island.

A community business group is now speeding up development.

Activities

Exercises

1. Fill in the blanks in the following passage.

   Pataku Island is located 200 kilometres __________ __________ of Manus Island, and is part of a __________ __________. The soil is __________ and is not good for growing __________. From April to __________ the seas are usually __________. This is the time when most of the islanders go __________. From October to __________ the seas are too rough for __________. Instead the islanders harvest clams from the __________ at the __________ end of the Island.

2. Copy the following table into your exercise book and complete it by:
   (a) listing all the activities the people of Pakatu do together
   (b) giving the reasons for doing each activity.

(a) ACTIVITIES	(b) REASONS

3. Copy and complete the chart below by writing down what people do with the money they earn from the plantation.

INCOME FROM THE PLANTATION		

Things to discuss

1. Discuss the problems the people on Pataku would have in:
   (a) obtaining fresh water
   (b) finding firewood
   (c) obtaining good medical services.
   How might the people solve these problems?
2. Imagine you lived on Pataku Island.
   (a) Would you want to leave the island and go to high school?
   (b) What would you do for your village if you completed high school?
3. Discuss why *sharing* is so important in isolated communities.

Things to do

1. Using the *Jacaranda Papua New Guinea School Atlas*, pages 8 and 9, locate the Ninigo group of islands.
   (a) What is the latitude of the Ninigo group?
   (b) What is the longitude?
   (c) How far away is Wewak from the Ninigo group, and in what direction.
   (d) Draw a map of Manus Province and show the Ninigo group. Label: Lorengau, Momote Airport and the Bismarck Sea. Make sure you include a scale and a direction rose.
2. Find out what copra is. Write a paragraph to describe how copra is made. Make a list of the things that copra is used for.

3. Rural Communities: The Somali of North-East Africa

Environment

The Somali people live in north-east Africa. Most live in Somalia.

The climate of north-east Africa is mainly hot and dry, and the Somali identify three seasons in the year.

- The main dry season (*jillal*) is from December to March.
- The main wet season (*gu*) is from April to July.
- The season of light rains *(der)* is from August to November.

The wind blows from the north-east all the year. This wind travels across large areas of desert before it reaches Somalia and so it is very dry. The vegetation does not benefit very much from the rainy season. The days are so hot (often over 40°C) that any rain which falls dries up (evaporates) very quickly.

Map of Africa showing the prevailing winds and some main countries.

The vegetation is sparse (thinly scattered). It consists of short tuft grasses and scattered, stunted trees. This type of vegetation is called **dry savanna.**

The climate graphs below are for Mogadishu, the capital city of Somalia. The city is only 2km north of the equator.

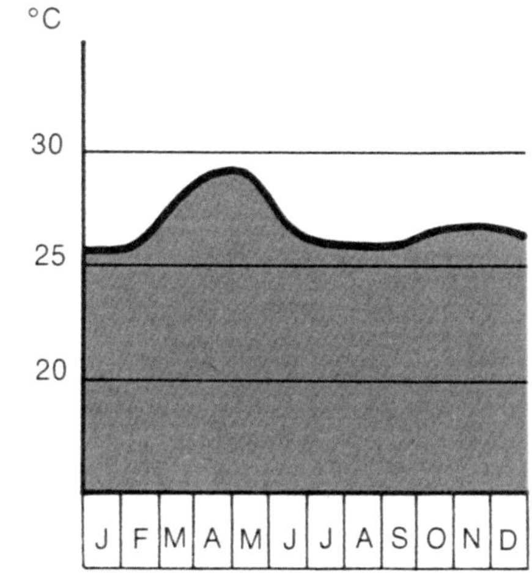

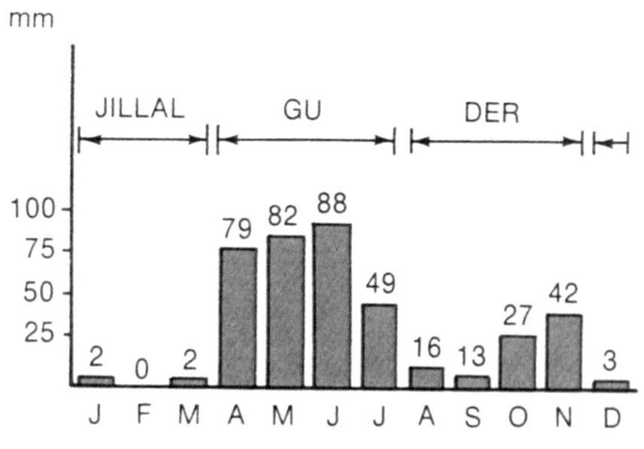

Temperature and rainfall graphs for Mogadishu (seasons are indicated).

Resources

The climate of Somalia is too dry in most places for people to grow crops. Instead, the people look after herds of camels and flocks of sheep and goats. Seventy per cent of people make their living in this way.

Nomadic herding

Water and pastures are the most important resources of the Somali. However, both of these resources are very limited because of the dry climate. The grass is poor and the animals quickly eat everything in one place. The Somali must move from place to place to find enough food and water for their herds. Throughout the year, the Somali move along carefully selected routes which provide enough vegetation and water for their animals. This way of life is called nomadic herding. A nomad is a person who has no fixed place to live and moves from place to place to make a living.

Meeting their needs

The Somali way of life is linked very closely to their animals. The sheep and goats provide the herdsmen and their families with meat and milk. The hides (skins) are usually used to build shelters. The Somali earn money by selling some of their animals for export.

Camels are particularly important. They provide transport for each family's possessions. The size of the camel herd gives status within the community.

Shelter

The nomads' shelters are made by stretching animal skins over a framework of curved saplings (young trees). This shelters people from the heat of the day. The animal-skin covering keeps the inside of the shelter cool. When the Somali move, the tent is packed on the back of a camel and carried to the next camping place.

1 Like many nomadic peoples, Somali nomads must constantly move to seek new grazing for their herds. They carry their household by camel.

2 The framework of the house is made from curved saplings tied together with bark and twine. The house is held in position by pushing saplings into the ground.

3 The women, who do all the construction, then attach animal skins to the frame.

4 The completed tent takes about two hours to put up. Nomad groups may move every few days. It is cool and well insulated by mats, which can be lifted to let in a breeze.

Somali shelter erection.

Cash income

At the end of the dry season many nomads gather near Hargeisa and Burao (see map). The land is higher there and the climate is cooler and wetter. Local farmers sell hay and sorghum to the nomads to fatten the stock (their animals). Traders come here to buy the animals. The animals are then taken by truck to Berbera to be exported, mainly to Saudi Arabia.

Organisation

Not all Somali live in Somalia. The map shows that there are nomadic Somali who live in the neighbouring countries of Djibuti, Ethiopia and Kenya.

There are four main clans of Somali. Each clan has a homeland that it returns to once each year. Within each clan there are groups of people who travel together in search of new pastures. Each group contains about 30 to 40 families.

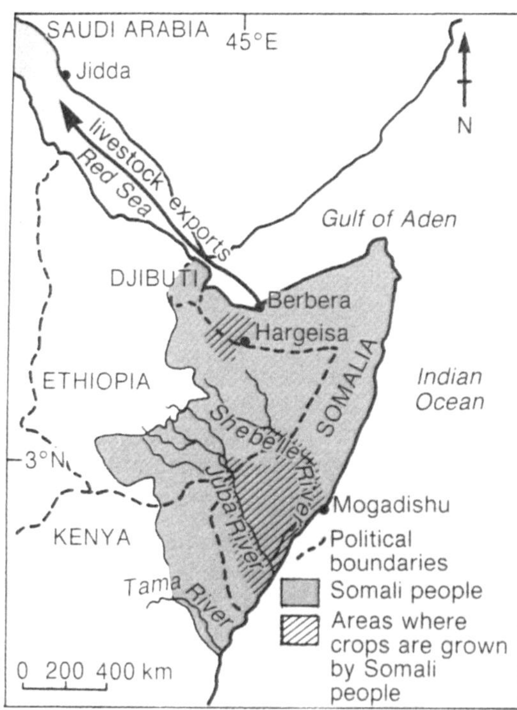

Somalia and neighbouring countries.

Polygamy

A Somali man is allowed to have up to four wives. There are many children. Many young Somali children die in the harsh conditions of the dry savanna. Each wife has a separate shelter and looks after her own flock of sheep and goats.

Family roles

Men and women have different roles in these nomadic communities. From the age of seven until he marries, a male looks after camels. This is a very important job as camels are given high status. After he is married, a man joins the women and helps to look after the herds of sheep and goats. The girls stay with their mothers and learn how to cook, put up the shelters and load the camels. They also look after the sheep and goats.

The head of the family makes all the decisions about where to move next. His judgement is very important as the herds must have a regular supply of food and water.

Summary

The environment of the Somali is hot and dry.

The Somali are **nomadic herders** — they travel with all their possessions, and look after sheep, goats and camels.

The Somali are nomads because there is not enough rainfall to support rich pastures for their herds.

The Somali earn a cash income by selling some of their sheep and goats for export.

Males and females have different **roles:**

- boys look after the camels
- men move with the herds of sheep and goats
- girls and women cook and look after the sheep and goats.

Activities

Exercises

1. Fill in the blanks in the following passage.

   Somalia is situated in the north-east of the continent of __________. The climate is very __________ and __________. This is because the wind blows across the __________ before reaching Somalia. The Somali people are __________ __________. They travel across the countryside looking for fresh supplies of __________ and __________ for their animals. They herd flocks of __________ and herds of __________. Their most important animal is the __________. The size of a man's camel herd gives him __________ within the community.

2. Complete the table below to show the different roles of men and women in Somali society.

PERSON	ROLE
Unmarried boy	
Unmarried girl	
Married man	
Married woman	

3. Complete the table below to show what each animal gives to the Somali community and what each product is used for.

ANIMAL	PRODUCT	USE
Sheep	Meat Wool	
Goats	Milk Skins	
Camels	Milk Skins Transport Status	

Things to discuss

1. Discuss the difference between polygamy and monogamy. What advantages might polygamy have in a difficult environment like Somalia?
2. Imagine you are a nomadic leader. Discuss the most important things you would need to carry with you.

Things to do

1. Look at the map of Africa in the *Jacaranda Papua New Guinea School Atlas*, page 42.
   (a) What is the latitude and longitude of Mogadishu?
   (b) Name two countries sharing borders with Somalia.
   (c) What is the name of the sea to the north of Somalia?
   (d) What is the name of the ocean to the east of Somalia?
   (e) Complete the following table to show the distance and direction of each city from Mogadishu, and the country each is situated in.

CITY	DISTANCE	DIRECTION	COUNTRY
Nairobi Djibouti Capetown Cairo Harare Kinshasa Baghdad			

4. Rural Communities: A Rural Village in South-West India

In this chapter we will study a rural community called Punnayurkalam in India. The community is one of the many small villages in Kerala State, a densely populated region in south-west India. India is a very large country in South-East Asia with a population of over 700 million people. The map shows the location of the village in India.

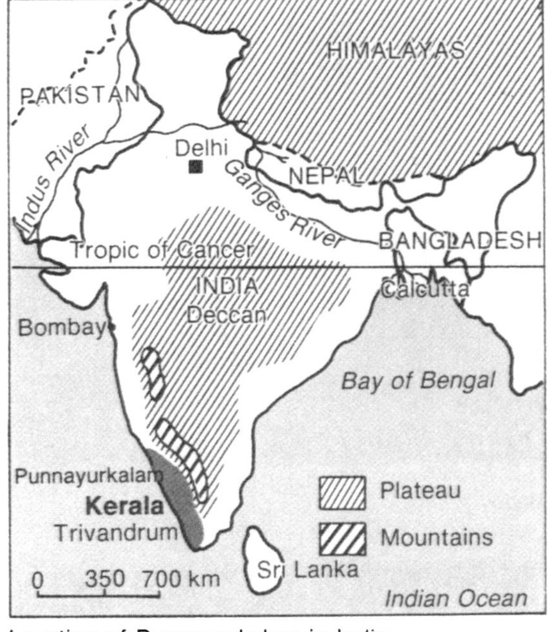

Location of Punnayurkalam in India.

Environment

The climate is hot and wet (tropical). There are two seasons in the year. The winds of this region blow from two different directions; the direction determines the season. These winds are the monsoon winds.

Between November and May the wind blows from the north-east. This is the 'dry' season, although there are occasional thunderstorms. In June the wind direction suddenly changes to come from the south-west. This wind brings heavy rain to most of India. This rain is very important to the lives of most Indian people.

The climate graphs show the variation in rainfall and temperature throughout the year.

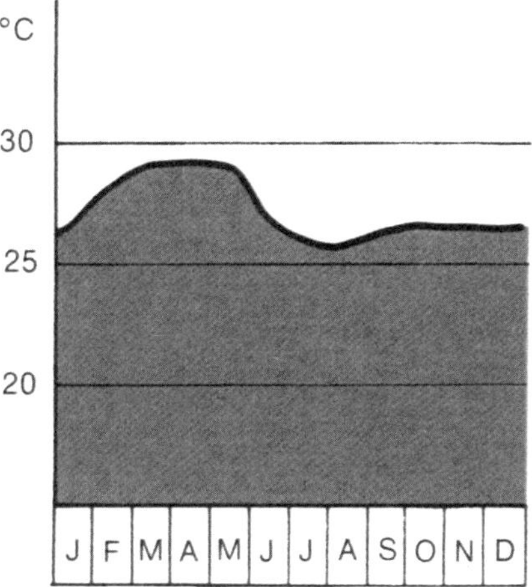

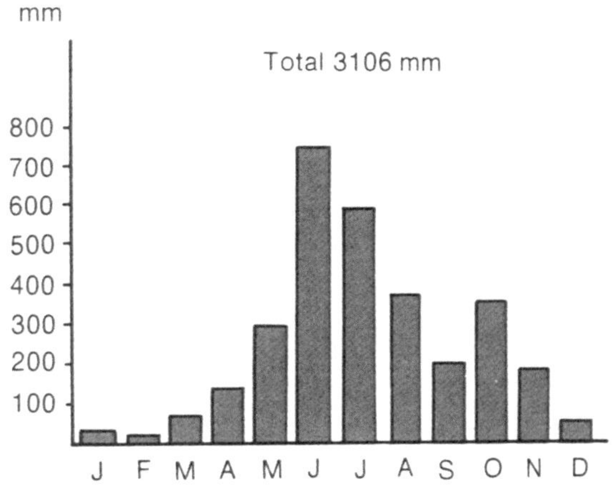

Temperature and rainfall graphs for Punnayurkalam.

Resources

Rice

The main food crop of the people in Punnayurkalam is rice. This is their staple food. In the dry months before the monsoon rains arrive, many labourers from the village prepare special fields, called **padi**, for the local landowners. The padi fields have low banks around them so that when the rains come they quickly become flooded.

From March to May rice seedlings are grown in special nursery gardens. This protects them from pests and diseases. The monsoon rains usually arrive on 1 June and the seedlings are planted in the flooded padis. If the rains are late then the padis are flooded from water channels. This use of water channels is called **irrigation.**

Ploughing a padi field. Inset shows detail of a rice plant.

The rains lessen and stop during October, and the sun appears more and more often. The sun ripens the grain. When the grain is ripe the banks of the padis are broken to let the water drain out. Women labourers from the village then come to harvest the rice. They do this by cutting off the stalks of the rice with a sickle. The harvested rice is tied into bundles and carried to the main house of the landowner. The women tread on the rice stalks to separate the grains of rice from their protective coverings (called husks). This is called threshing,

Harvesting rice.

and the labourers are paid one-sixth of all the rice they thresh.

Rice is the staple crop of all countries in South-East Asia. It is a type of grass, like wheat, oats, millet and corn. Cultivated (grown by people) grasses such as these are called cereals.

To grow well, rice needs:

- a hot, wet climate
- at least 1000 mm rain each year
- moist (flooded), fertile soils
- a short, sunny, dry period to ripen the grain
- flat land, such as a river delta or a wide river valley.

In mountainous areas people grow rice by building flat terraces on the hillsides.

Threshers.

Often, when the threshing is finished, the very poor people of the village come and pick any grains of rice left behind by the threshers. These people are called gleaners. They survive only on whatever rice they collect.

Cash crops

Rice is not the only food crop grown by the landowners. They also grow coconuts, tapioca, bananas and vegetables. Some of these are used as food for their households. The surplus is sold at the markets. The landowners employ servants to look after the food gardens.

Most of the landowners' income comes from cash crops. Cashew nuts, cocoa and especially peppers are very profitable. The high income from these crops means that the landowners are able to live in large houses and to employ servants to look after them. Another benefit is that they are able to employ many labourers from the village to grow the rice.

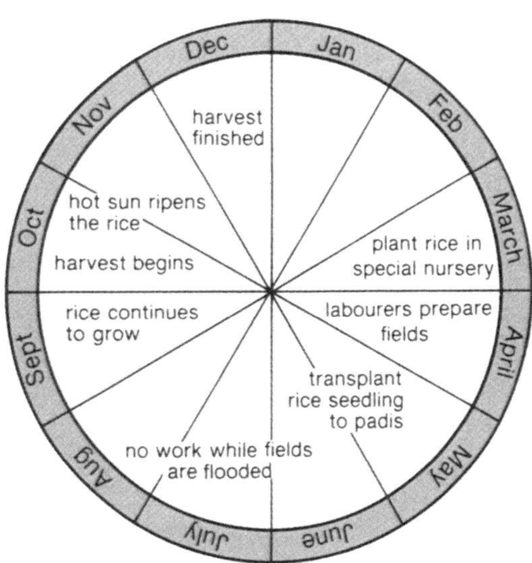

Pie chart showing what is done to grow rice each year.

Organisation

Social status

In the past, there were great differences between people in the village. People in Indian societies were separated into very different groups, called **castes**. The lowest caste of people were the untouchables, sometimes called *harijans*. They had no rights and were not allowed to mix with people of higher status. Nowadays they have the same rights as everyone else. However, because they are poor, they do not have any luxuries. Many of them now own a small plot of land, and their own houses—simple square buildings of brick and clay with thatched (grass) roofs. They grow their own vegetables to eat on the limited land they own. However, they need to work as labourers to buy meat and fish from the market and to clothe and educate their children. About 50 per cent of the village people are labourers.

The middle class of people are the **artisans**: goldsmiths, fisherfolk, carpenters and plumbers, etc. They earn more money than the lowest class of people because of the skills they have learned. The people who have the most wealth are the landowners or *nair*.

The diagram shows the social structure of the village.

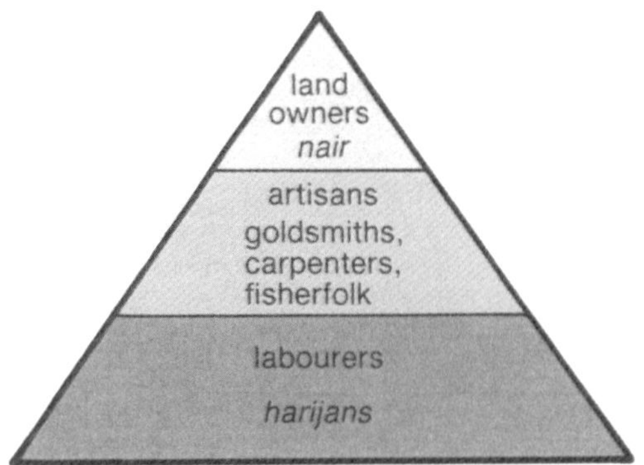

The structure of Indian society.

Politics

An elected council administers the affairs of the village. The council is responsible to a District Officer. There are 10 districts in Kerala State, administered by an elected state government. The state government has been trying to reform land ownership in recent years. It has succeeded in distributing land more fairly amongst all classes of people.

Education

Education is very important to all the people in the village. The lower-caste families can now afford to send their children to school. They all hope they will get jobs when they leave school and that this may improve their status. However, even university graduates have difficulty in finding employment in India today.

Village shops.

There are several small schools for pupils up to grade 6, but only one for grades 7 to 10. Many students must leave school early, and there is great competition for places in the secondary school. School classes are very crowded, with up to 60 students in one class. This makes it difficult to learn properly.

Services

There were no sealed roads in the village of Punnayurkalam until 1960, and even today few people visit the State capital. People use taxis or buses when they want to travel to nearby areas. Very few people own a car.

The village has a variety of shops. There are different shops selling clothes, shoes, groceries, hardware, medical supplies and jewellery. This **specialisation** means that many people can own shops without too much competition from others.

There are three main religions practised in Punnayurkalam—Christian, Hindu and Muslim. There are many buildings where people gather for religious ceremonies (e.g. churches and mosques), and people are free to practise the religion of their choice.

The map shows the location of some of the services in Punnayurkalam.

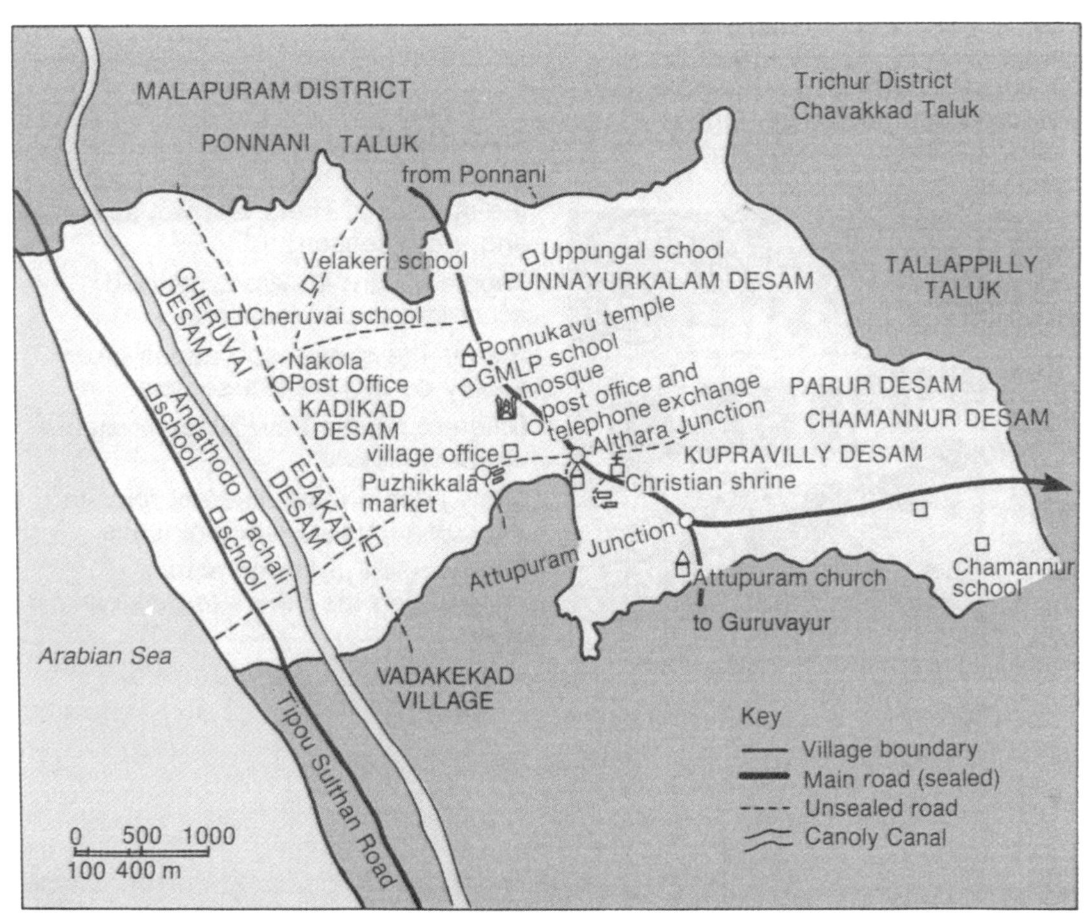

Punnayurkalam village.

Interdependence

Much of the economy of Punnayurkalam depends on farming. The few rich landowners provide work and wages for over half the people in the village. In turn, the landowners depend on the labourers to look after and harvest their crops.

The money that people earn is used to buy food, clothing and utensils. The shopowners depend on the labourers to spend their wages in their shops. If the people have no work, they have no money and the shopowners cannot make a living.

This is interdependence (inter = between), or dependence between people.

Everyone in the village society has a role to play. Some people have different roles at different times. For example, some landowners are also village councillors. They have to supervise their fields and families, as well as doing their official duties.

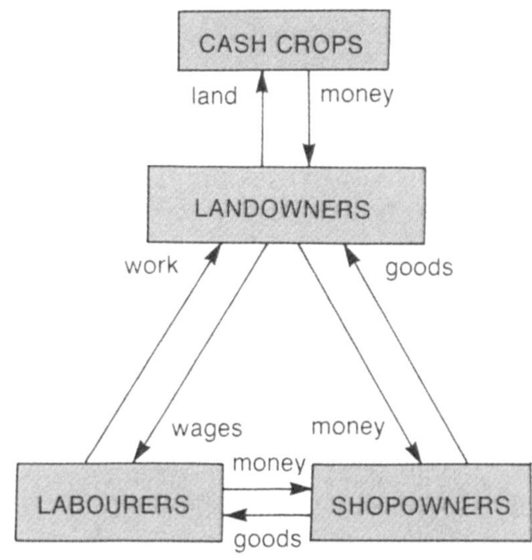

Interdependence.

People buying goods at the village shops.

Summary

The climate of India is influenced by the monsoon. There is a wet season and a dry season.

People's activities are organised according to the seasons.

Rice is the staple food and is grown mainly during the wet season.

Different people have different status in the community.

Many people have different roles in the community at different times.

Each person in the community depends on the others to make a living.

Activities

Exercises

1. Fill in the blanks in the following passage.

   Punnayurkalam is situated in __________ State in __________-__________ India.

   The climate is influenced mainly by the __________ winds. From __________ to __________ the winds blow from the north-east. During this time there is not a lot of __________. Between June and October the winds blow from the __________-__________. During this season the winds bring heavy __________. This climate is very good for growing __________, which is the __________ crop of this region.

2. Copy the following table into your exercise book. It shows how much rice was produced by different countries in 1983.
   - **(a)** Draw a column graph to show the information given in the table.
   - **(b)** Work out the percentage of the total that each country produces, and complete the table.
   - **(c)** Draw a pie graph to show the proportion of the world total rice production produced by each country.
   - **(d)** List all the countries in order of rice production from greatest to smallest.

3. Imagine you are a farm labourer in India. Write a paragraph to describe your work through the different seasons of the year.

Things to discuss

1. Compare the structure of Indian society (diagram on page 24) with the structure of your own home society. Make a list of any similarities or differences.
2. Discuss the importance of the monsoon to the way the people live in Punnayurkalam.
   Imagine that the monsoon did not arrive one year. What would be the effect on:
   - **(a)** the labourers
   - **(b)** artisans
   - **(c)** landowners?

COUNTRY	PRODUCTION	% OF TOTAL
India	72 million tonnes	
Bangladesh	15 million tonnes	
Burma	9 million tonnes	
Thailand	12 million tonnes	
Indonesia	24 million tonnes	
China	113 million tonnes	
Japan	10 million tonnes	
United States	4 million tonnes	
Brazil	6 million tonnes	
TOTAL	350 million tonnes	100

Things to do

1. Study the diagram on page 26 showing the interdependence of people living in Punnayurkalam. Draw a similar diagram to show how people from your home society depend on each other.
2. The monsoon often causes problems for people living in South Asia. Collect newspaper cuttings about droughts and floods in India, Pakistan and Bangladesh.
3. Write a paragraph to explain how monsoon winds affect Papua New Guinea. How different are the seasons caused by monsoon winds in your area?

5. Rural Communities: A Small Village in England

In this chapter we will study a community found in a region with a temperate climate. In temperate latitudes seasonal differences in temperature often create problems for the people who live there. Sometimes communities become temporarily isolated because of bad weather. We will see how this community in England organises itself to cope with the environment.

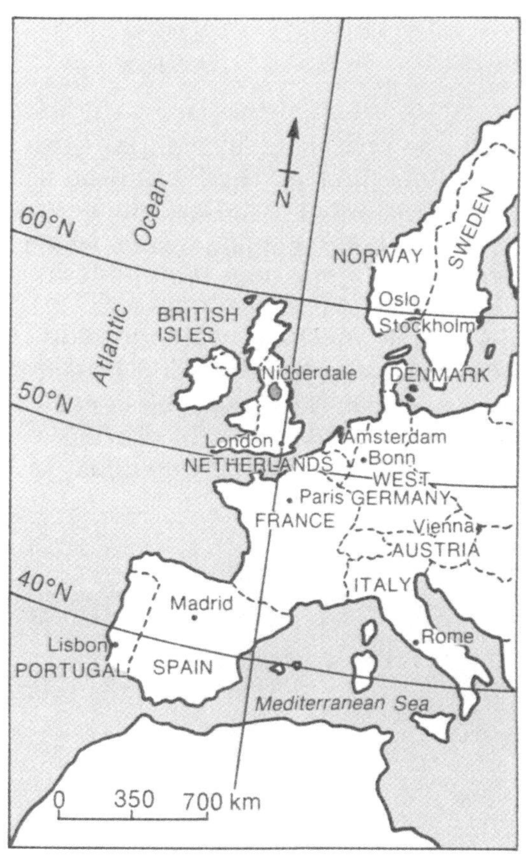

North-west Europe and the British Isles.

Environment

The British Isles are in north-west Europe. They are made up of four countries, England, Scotland, Wales and Ireland. The village in this case study is in an area in the north of England known as Yorkshire. The maps locate these places.

The climate changes a lot from one part of the year to another. There are four seasons.

- Summer is quite warm.
- Autumn is cool and misty, and is the time when many trees lose their leaves.
- Winter is cold and snow often covers the ground.
- Spring is the warmer season after winter, and is the time when plants begin to grow again.

Rain falls all through the year, although not as much as in Papua New Guinea.

Nidderdale is a valley (dale = valley) that runs from the high land (Pennine Hills) in the centre of England to the east coast. The high rainfall on these hills causes many small streams to flow downhill to the lowlands. One of these streams is the Nidd. The Nidd flows eastward, passing through the villages of Pately Bridge and Glasshouses before it eventually joins the River Ouse near York. You can follow the course of the river on the map.

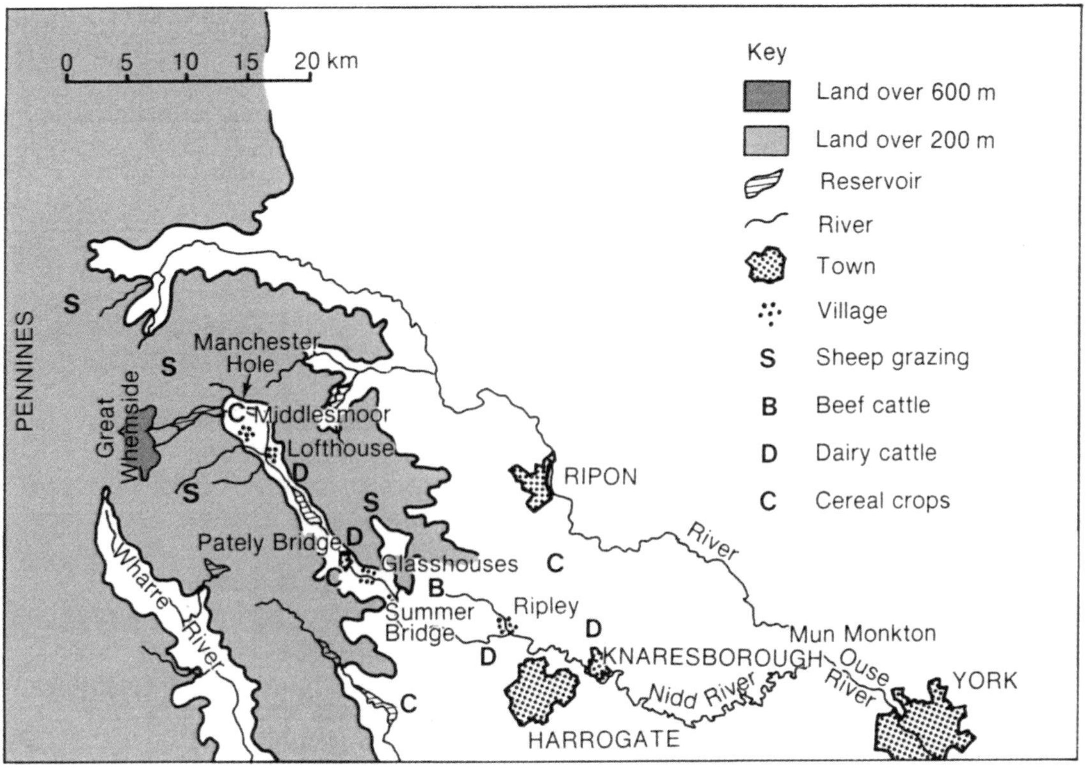

0 5 10 15 20 km

Key

Land over 600 m
Land over 200 m
Reservoir
River
Town
Village
S Sheep grazing
B Beef cattle
D Dairy cattle
C Cereal crops

PENNINES
Great Whernside
Manchester Hole
Middlesmoor
Lofthouse
Pately Bridge
Glasshouses
Summer Bridge
Wharre River
Ripley
RIPON
River
Mun Monkton
KNARESBOROUGH
Nidd River
Ouse River
YORK
HARROGATE

Nidderdale.

Nidderdale, looking downstream towards Gouthwaite Reservoir.

Resources

Many settlements in England are near water. Glasshouses is a small village in Nidderdale. It was started because a mill was built there. In the past water power from the river Nidd was used to turn the mill-wheel. The mill-wheel turned two large grinding stones which were used to grind flour from the cereal crops of the local farmers. When steam machines were invented about 150 years ago the mill gradually fell into disuse. Nowadays the land in the valley is used mainly for grazing cattle. Sheep graze on the uplands.

The old mill at Glasshouses.

Mill and grinding stones.

Lack of resources in the valley has meant that the population of the village has not grown very much. The only people who live in Glasshouses now are a few farmers and some people who run a small factory in the old mill. Some people drive to work in the nearby big town, Harrogate. Several, old, retired people also live in the village.

Organisation

Mobile services

Mrs Wilkinson has lived in the village of Glasshouses all her life. She is 80 years old now and finds difficulty in walking very far. She can remember when the village was very small. She lives in a row of houses joined together (called a terrace). They were first built for the mill workers and are still occupied. There is only one shop in Glasshouses. This is the Post Office, which also has a small section for selling chocolate and cigarettes. The nearest food shops are at Pately Bridge, a larger town about 3 kilometres away.

The Post Office at Middlesmoor.

How do the old people manage to get their food supplies? Many people would help if it was needed. However it is not becuase many of the villages in Nidderdale are served by mobile shops. Mr Weatherhead, for example, sells meat (beef, lamb and pork) and pies from the back of his van. His family started the business more than 100 years ago. Then, they used to carry their goods by a horse and cart. Now, to increase the number of customers, Mr Weatherhead drives from village to village selling his produce in his van. He also has a shop in Pately Bridge.

Mr Weatherhead and his mobile butcher shop.

Many people in isolated villages in Nidderdale depend on the mobile shops for their survival. The mobile shops depend on the villagers for their trade. The mobile shops are particularly important in winter when the weather is cold and wet. Mrs Wilkinson, like many others in the village, prefers to stay in her house at this time.

Groceries also are delivered by a mobile shop. The shop visits only once or twice a week and so people must buy a lot of food and store it at home. Milk and dairy products are delivered to every house every day, and the postman sometimes delivers letters twice each day. The library of Harrogate also sends out a bus so that people can borrow books.

This mobile shop service is very useful to the community. Although the village is isolated from the large centres all the resources the people need are brought to them.

Mobile grocer's van.

Co-operation

In the summer a local farmer cuts the grass on the open space in the middle of the village. This keeps the village looking tidy. He also stores the grass on his farm to feed his animals when the ground is covered in snow. In return for keeping the village tidy, the villagers help him dig the snow when his tracks are blocked in winter. This **co-operation** helps everyone.

A farmer cutting grass on the village green.

Transport

Buses go from Glasshouses to Pately Bridge and Harrogate (see map) every day. There is also a footpath to Pately Bridge alongside the river but it is often blocked by the snow in winter. It also becomes slippery when it rains in summer. In the winter, the roads to Pately Bridge and Harrogate are often completely blocked by snow. The villages in Nidderdale are then completely cut off from their services. When their supplies begin to run out, emergency food and mail are flown to them by helicopter.

The bus station at Harrogate.

Maintaining links

Although Glasshouses is a small and isolated community, a regular system of mobile shops and public transport ensures they have good links with larger centres. The larger centres understand the problems of the isolated villages and have extended their services so that all people feel part of the larger community. When conditions are bad, no one is forgotten. Extra efforts are made to ensure that people do not suffer.

Snowbound cars.

Summary

Many communities in England are located close to rivers.

The main resources of rural communities in England are the rivers and the land.

Rural communities are small and often isolated from services.

Mobile services supply rural communities with most of the things people need and want.

When conditions are severe (bad), **emergency services** from nearby urban centres are used to ensure that rural people can survive.

Activities

Exercises

1. Fill in the blanks in the following passage.

   The British Isles have a__________ climate. There are four __________ in the year. The warmest season is called __________. In winter it is cold and __________ often covers the ground. There are many rivers in the British Isles because __________ falls all through the year.

2. Answer the following questions.
   (a) In which season do many trees lose their leaves?
   (b) When do the trees begin to grow new leaves?
   (c) What are communities that are a long way from resources and services called?
   (d) Why was Glasshouses built next to the river Nidd?

3. Study the map of north-west Europe on page 29.
   (a) What direction is Rome from London?
   (b) How far is it from Oslo to Stockholm?
   (c) What is the latitude of Nidderdale?
   (d) What is the name of the ocean to the west of the British Isles?
   (e) Copy out and complete the following table by writing in the country or the name of the capital city.

COUNTRY	CAPITAL CITY
Spain	
	Lisbon
	Rome
France	
West Germany	
	Amsterdam

Things to discuss

1. Discuss the benefits of mobile shops to people living in the rural areas. Would mobile shops be a good idea for places in Papua New Guinea?
2. Do the mobile shops provide all the villagers' needs and wants? Where would the people have to go to obtain new clothes, a high school education, medical treatment or a new car?
3. How does co-operation benefit the people of Nidderdale?

Things to do

1. Collect pictures from magazines to show the differences between the four seasons in Europe. Make a poster to show how farmers' activities change throughout the year.
2. Write a paragraph to describe how people's activities in Papua New Guinea change according to the two seasons.
3. Find out about emergency services in Papua New Guinea. Make a list of the natural disasters that may occur in Papua New Guinea to cause people to need help, e.g. volcanic eruption.
4. Collect newspaper clippings that describe occasions when emergency services have been used in Papua New Guinea.

6. Urban Communities: Port Moresby

The Growth of an Urban Area

A settlement develops into an urban area when more and more people come to live there. The original community is joined by people from other communities. Often, the new arrivals live together with people from their own background. For example, within a large Australian city such as Sydney there are many separate communities. These communities are from different countries, such as Greece, Italy, Turkey, Vietnam or Chile.

In the next three chapters we will study three types of community in Port Moresby: the urban villages, the migrant settlements, and the business community of the city itself.

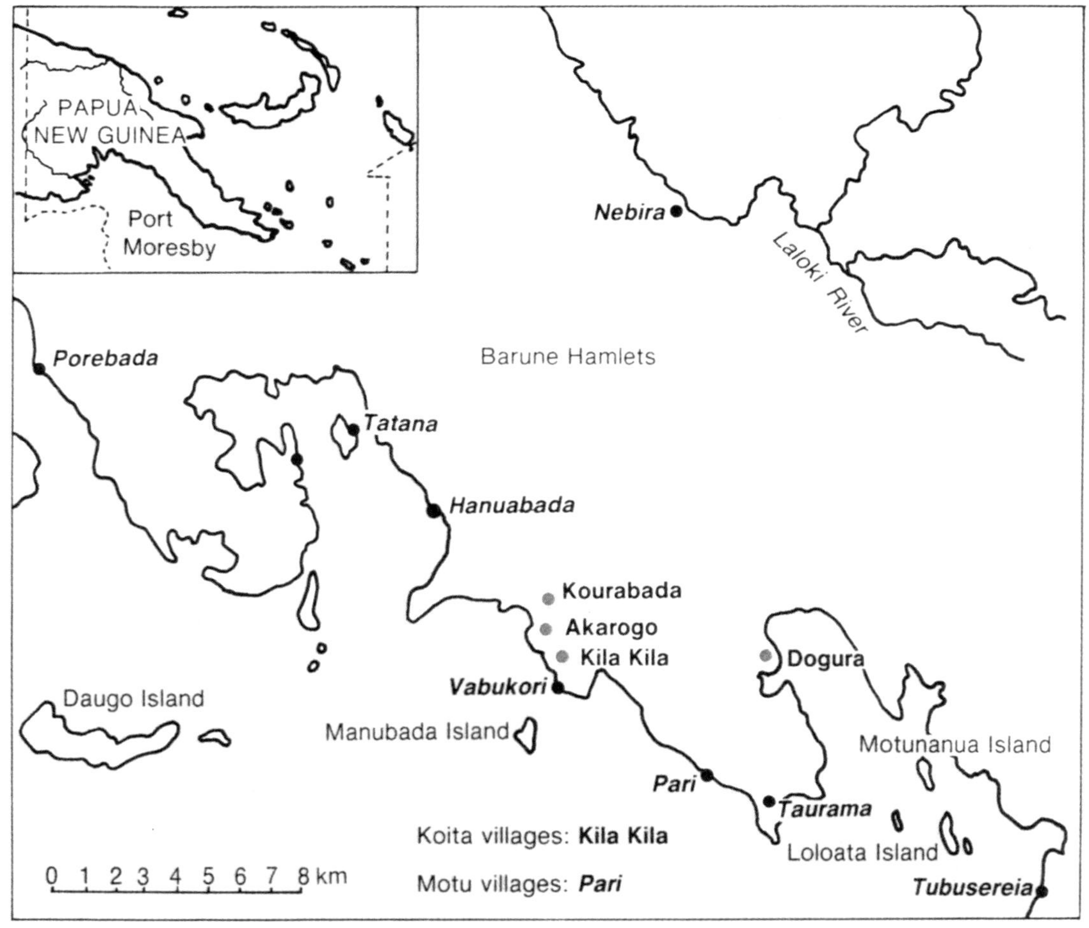

Moresby and Motu/Koita villages in 1873.

Urban Villages

The capital city of Papua New Guinea, and largest urban centre, is Port Moresby. In 1877 the area was described by one of the first foreign visitors, the Rev. Chalmers, as being unhealthy and swampy. There were two groups of people already living there, the Motuans and the Koita people, numbering only about 800 people. Now Port Moresby has a population of over 120 000 people (1980 census) and is the main commercial and administrative centre of the country.

Before European contact

Motu villages consisted of houses built on stilts over the water on the coast. Their houses had walls and roofs made of nipa thatch. The Motu villagers lived by fishing and hunting bush wallabies in the grassland near their villages. They also grew some bananas, taro, sweet potato and yams on the infertile soil near their villages. Their most important activity was the Hiri trade. The Motuans sailed their large double-hulled canoes along the coast, trading their pottery for sago with the people of the Gulf of Papua.

Hiri Lakatoi near Elevala in 1885.

Inland, on the tops of the ridges that run parallel to the coast, were the villages of the Koita people. They built their houses here to make them easy to defend. Because of this they were a long way from fresh water. By the time the first Europeans arrived, the Motu and Koita people had already intermarried to a large extent.

All children were taught, by their families, the skills and social behaviour they needed to live in the villages. They learned the activities associated with the different seasons, gardening, fishing, hunting and the Hiri expedition. They were also taught how to handle relationships with people who had particular roles to play in the community. Respect for family elders and generosity towards kinsmen were particularly important values.

The First Europeans

Captain John Moresby was the first foreigner to sail through the gap in the main reef, into what he called Moresby Harbour. He anchored close to the village of Hanuabada on 20 February 1873.

Early view of Hanuabada from Elevala with LMS station behind.

The first foreign settlers in the area were from the London Missionary Society. They built their mission close to Hanuabada in 1875, and by 1885 had become firmly established all along the Papuan coast. The influence of these early missionaries, especially the Reverend Lawes, is still strong in these villages today.

Raising the British flag in 1884.

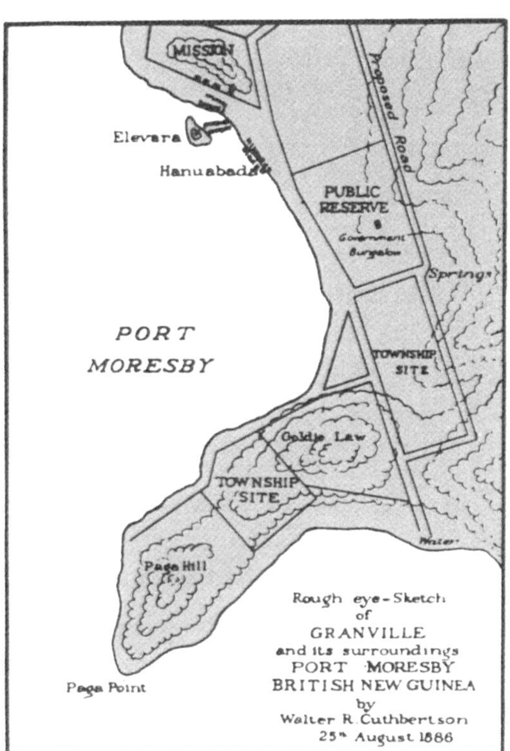

Cuthbertson's map of Port Moresby, 1886.

In 1884 the Papuan region of Papua New Guinea was declared a British Protectorate. The colonial powers made firm plans to develop Port Moresby as the capital city and administrative centre of the region. They laid down regulations for the behaviour of the villagers and the colonists. The traditional lives of the villagers around Port Moresby changed a lot because of these laws and Christianity.

Growth and development

In 1906 Britain handed over the administration of Papua to the Australian government. Australian trading companies, such as Burns Philp and Steamships, were building stores and warehouses. Local villagers were able to find employment in the town as labourers and as domestic servants to the foreigners. However, they were not allowed to live in the same parts of town as the white settlers.

Burns Philp and Company in Port Moresby in 1897.

The growth of Port Moresby was very slow. By 1941 there were only 400 Europeans living there.

During the Second World War the Motuan and Koita villagers were sent to villages along the coast where they made close links with the people there. This was a time of great hardship. The traditional nipa palm houses of the Motu-Koita people fell

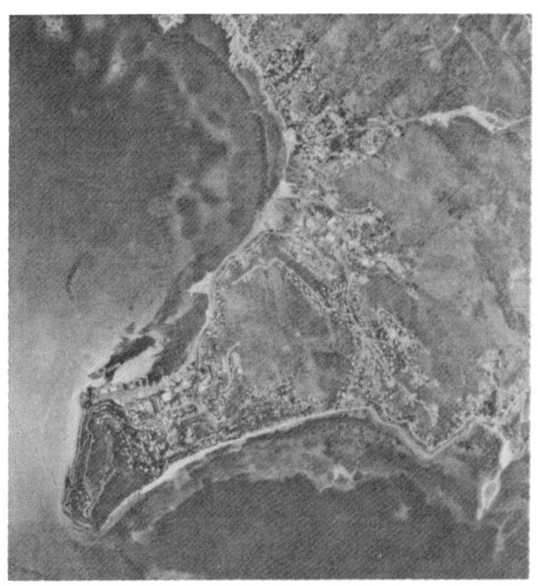
Aerial photograph of Port Moresby in 1960.

into disrepair and many of the children died from lack of food. However, when the people returned after the war they found many kilometres of army tracks which improved their links with neighbouring villages and the capital. The Australian army rebuilt Hanuabada with longer-lasting wooden houses. The Koita people moved off their hills and settled on the sites of old army camps which had the advantage of nearby water. They also used much of the wartime metal sheeting left behind by the army to build houses that were able to last much longer.

New houses in post-war Hanuabada.

Since the war, development in these villages has been rapid. Port Moresby has continued to grow as an administrative and commercial centre. The Motu-Koita villages took advantage of the urban services that were becoming available. They all now have electricity and piped water. They have health centres and schools. Their populations have increased enormously while the rest of Port Moresby has expanded and grown around them. These urban villages have remained separate from the modern urban development. At the same time they have benefited from the urban services. However, they have also suffered many of the problems that develop in urban areas.

Change

The life-style of the people who live in the urban village communities is now very different from that of 1873. The change that has taken place is the process of urbanisation. Communities that depended on the resources of the countryside have changed to communities that depend on the services and resources of a large town.

Port Moresby today with Hanuabada in foreground.

Very few villagers still practise the traditional activities of hunting, fishing, trading and gardening. Instead, many people have found work in the city and now buy their food from local supermarkets or tradestores. Much of the land that was once used for gardens is now used for new housing developments for the growing population of Port Moresby. Canoes are still built in the coastal villages, but the canoes are now used more for racing than for the traditional activities of fishing and trading. Those people who wish to fish on the main reef now use aluminium dinghies and outboard motors as their preferred means of transport.

The rapid growth of the urban village population has been caused partly by inward **migration** of people from outside the area. Many outsiders have come because of links established between the Motuans and the people they traded with during the Hiri expeditions. In Vabukori, which established trading links with both Goilala and Hula people, the immigrants now outnumber the original villagers.

Employment

Many urban villagers have been well educated and have risen to high positions in government departments throughout Papua New Guinea. The money they earn is put back into the village economy in the form of investment and new housing. This, in turn, has created jobs for skilled artisans such as carpenters. There are also small businesses which employ skilled tradesmen, particularly for repairing motor cars and outboard motors.

Small business in an urban village.

However, unemployment is becoming a serious problem. There are some youths who drop out of the education system. Without finishing their education they find it very hard to get a job. Traditional activities are no longer very important and there is little activity to occupy these youths. They are sometimes blamed for the increase in petty crime and rascal activities in the villages and in the city.

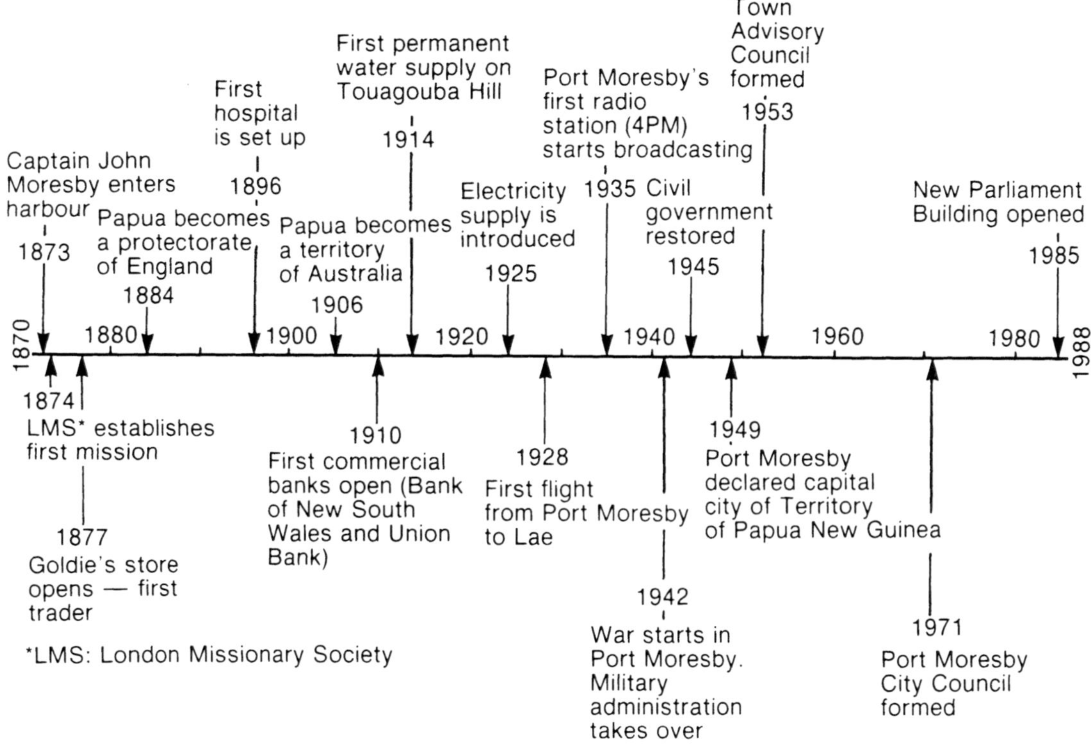

Timeline showing important events in Port Moresby 1873-1988.

Summary

The original inhabitants of the Port Moresby area were the Motu-Koita people.

The Motu-Koita were a rural community making a living by:

- subsistence gardening
- hunting and fishing
- trading by sea.

The traditional way of life of the Motu-Koita has been changed by the influence of:

- the London Missionary Society
- the British and Australian Colonial Administrations
- the Second World War
- the growth of Port Moresby since 1946 (urbanisation).

The original villages are now larger but still have a separate identity. They have gone through the process of urbanisation and are called urban villages.

The village economy is now more dependent on **employment** and money than on subsistence.

Activities

Exercises

1. Fill in the blanks in the following passage.

When more and more people come to live in a place it becomes an __________ area. Port Moresby is the __________ city of Papua New Guinea and is also the __________ urban centre. Port Moresby was first established in 1873 when Captain __________ sailed into the harbour. The original inhabitants of the area were the __________, living in houses on the coast, and the Koita who lived in villages on the __________ inland. Nowadays these villages are known as __________ villages because they have received many of the benefits of the development of the urban centre of __________ __________.

2. Copy the crossword below into your exercise books. Answer the clues and fill in the blank spaces.

CLUES

Across

1. The type of canoe used for trading voyages.
5. The initials of the first mission to settle in Port Moresby.
6. What people do to make sure that no one goes without food.
8 What Gulf people used to trade for pottery.
9. The palm used for roofing houses in Hanuabada.
12. The name given to places in the countryside.

Down

1. The leader of the first religious mission to Papua.
2. People living on ridges in the Port Moresby region.
3. What the Papuan people were originally.
4. The colonial power that took over the administration of Papua from Great Britain.
7. Coastal living people.
10. The name of a coastal village.
11. What came to Papua New Guinea in 1942.

Things to discuss

1. What aspects of urban life would be advantageous for a rural community?

2. Discuss the problems a rural community may face as it develops into an urban community. What would happen to:
(a) the status of village elders
(b) the traditional activities of the village
(c) family life?

Things to do

1. Most communities in Papua New Guinea have changed a great deal over the past 50 years. Find out how life is different now in your home area to the way people lived 50 years ago. Write two paragraphs to describe these changes and to explain why they have happened.
2. Draw a sketch of the photograph of Port Moresby and Hanuabada today on page 38. Label Port Moresby City, Port Moresby Harbour, Hanuabada and Elavala.

7. Urban Communities: Urban Migrant Settlements

Large cities in all developing countries have rapidly increasing populations. Much of this increase is due to large numbers of people leaving the rural areas and migrating to the cities. In many developing countries the rural areas are relatively poor. People think that the cities offer the chance of a better standard of living. The list below shows how some cities in the world are increasing in population.

CITY	POPULATION	URBAN SETTLERS
Mexico City	15 million	800 000 new settlers per year
Calcutta	7 million	over 1 million now live in slums
Manila	7 million	over 2 million now live in slums
Cairo	8 million	130 000 new settlers per year

In most developing countries there are not enough jobs for the thousands of people who move to the city each year. Without money or other resources, the migrants build shelters out of waste material on unused land near the city. Settlements like this are called slums, shanty towns or squatter settlements.

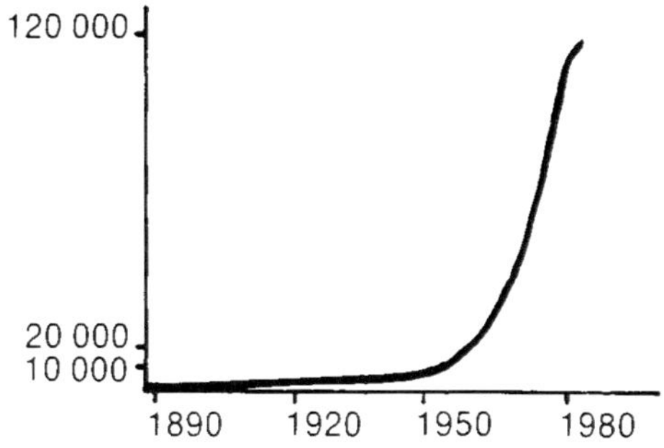

120 000
20 000
10 000
1890 1920 1950 1980

Graph of population growth of Port Moresby, 1888-1980.

Settlements in Port Moresby

After the Second World War in the Pacific, Port Moresby began to grow very quickly. Trade and commerce expanded and transport links with Australia and the rest of Papua New Guinea were improved. Many new buildings were put up and there was a demand for workers. Since the 1950s there has been a steady movement of people from the rural areas to Port Moresby. This movement is called rural-urban drift. The following table and graph show the population growth of Port Moresby between 1890 and 1980.

Growth of Population of Port Moresby 1947–1990	
YEAR	POPULATION
1947	7 230
1954	15 700
1961	29 000
1964	33 500
1966	41 850
1971	56 206
1975	111 300
1980	122 761
1985	136 300
1990	164 000 (est.)

Where do migrants come from?
Most settlers in Port Moresby are **migrants** from different parts of the country. Unlike the Motu and Koita people of the traditional villages around Port Moresby, they generally have no traditional land-rights in the area. Most of the settlers come from other places in the Papuan region, particularly the Gulf and Goilala areas. Others are from Hula and Wanigela in Central Province, and a few recent migrants are from Chimbu and Eastern Highlands. Very few have come from the New Guinea Islands and the Momase Region (Madang and Sepik provinces).

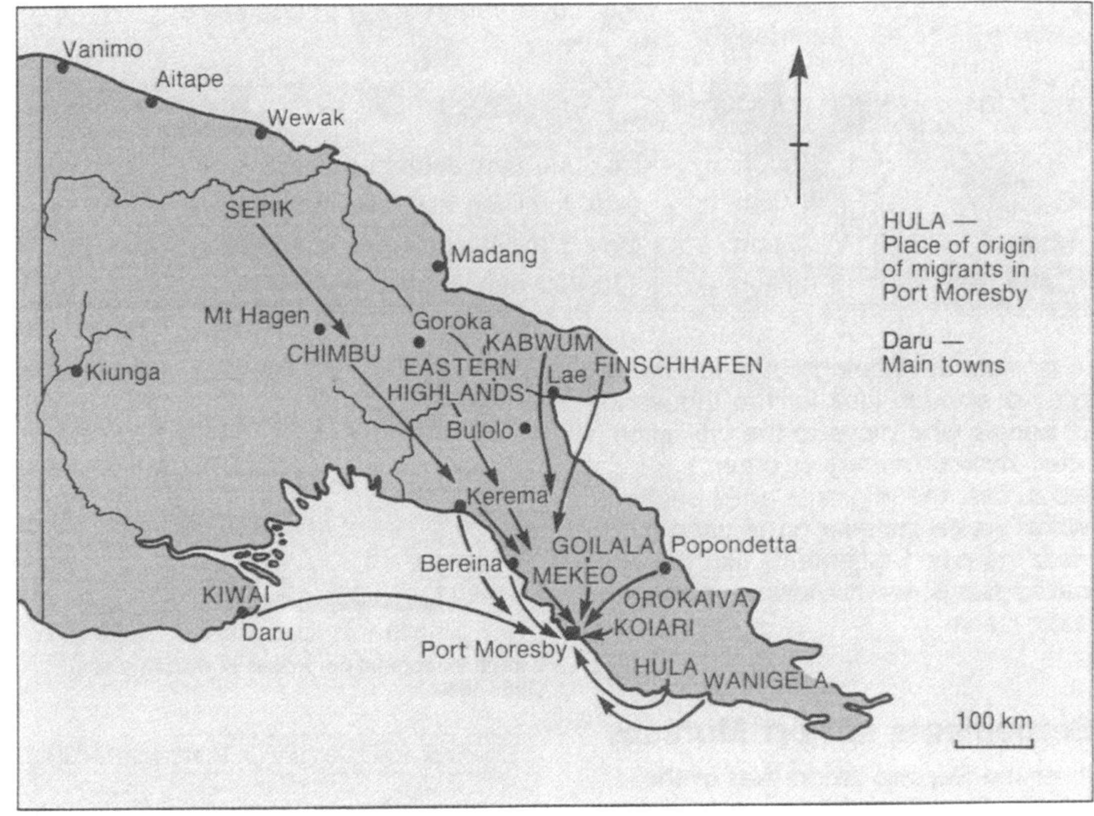

Origin of main settler groups in Port Moresby.

Why People Leave their Villages

There are many reasons why people move away from rural areas to urban centres.

Push factors
People often move away from their home area because conditions there become unsuitable. For example, some areas of Chimbu Province are overpopulated and the land cannot support all the people. In other areas, people have moved out because flooding, drought or some other natural disaster has destroyed their gardens and food crops. Some have even moved because of tribal conflicts. These things **push** people away from their own villages. Most travel to urban centres, particularly Port Moresby and

Lae, because they think they have a better chance of earning a living there.

Pull factors

Many people leave the rural areas because they are attracted by employment opportunities and the chance to earn more money. People who live in urban centres appear to enjoy a better standard of living and have better services (health care, education, etc.) than people in rural areas. Some are attracted by the 'bright lights' of the city, the bars, discos, cinemas and clubs. All of these attractions **pull** people from the villages to the big urban centres.

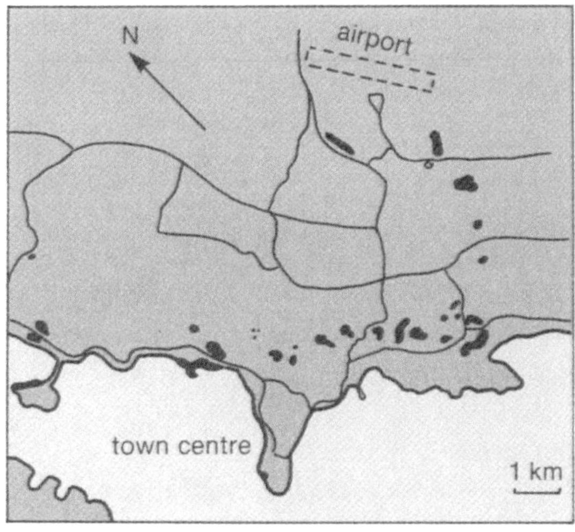

Migrant settlements in Port Moresby.

Resources

Land

Migrant settlers use land that is not wanted for development, such as steep slopes or swampy areas. In all cases, they settle as close as possible to work opportunities. The map above shows a crescent of settlements around the employment areas of the city. Where they have settled on customary land owned by urban villagers, settlers pay rent or give gifts to their landlords. Those that have settled on unused government land are now becoming more secure. In the past the government tried to control settlements and even made some settlers move. Nowadays, the government policy is to provide necessary services to the settlers to help them meet their needs and wants.

Shelter

When they first arrived, settlers built their shelters from any materials that they found locally. Many houses were built out of corrugated iron left behind after the War. Nowadays settlers use material from rubbish dumps or building site waste-tips. Some settlers have saved enough money to upgrade their houses with better materials.

Settlement houses.

The Wanigela settlement outside Port Moresby.

Earning a living

As in most developing countries there is not enough work for the thousands of people who move to the city each year. The situation is the same in Port Moresby. This means that most settlers must survive using their own skills. The Wanigela settlement at Koki is well known for its painters and decorators, and there is a cane-furniture workshop at the Koiari settlement on Gordon Ridge. Other settlers earn a living as bottle collectors, carvers, haus-meris, or general labourers.

Many settlers manage to earn a living by growing vegetables and selling them at the city markets. Even though the soil is poor, a lot of the vegetables grown in and around Port Moresby are grown by the settlers. They work very hard. Settlers who earn money share it with those settlers who are unemployed.

Cabbage gardens.

Bottle collection.

Organisation

Most settlers live in groups with people from their home areas, although each group of wantoks forms part of a larger community with groups from other areas. Most settlements have committees made up of the leaders of all the regional groups in the community. They meet regularly to discuss issues and problems that have arisen, and represent the community in its dealings with the city authorities. In some settlements there are peace officers and a village court system organised by the settlers.

Koiari furniture workshop.

Religion

Religion is important in settler areas all over the world. In Jakarta there are many mosques in the settlement areas. Almost all African settler areas

Settlement church.

have churches and Thai Buddhists build spirit houses in the slums of Bangkok.

Most settlements in Port Moresby have Christian churches, although the denominations vary from settlement to settlement. The settlers look after the churches themselves. The church acts as a central meeting point for most of the settler community.

Services

The Port Moresby City authorities have provided fresh-water standpipes to most of the settlement as part of a settlement upgrading programme. However, some communities have problems paying the bills as usage is very high. Access roads are being improved and the government provides financial and technical assistance for self-help house-upgrading projects. Some settlements have electricity supplied. However, not many people can afford to have it connected to their houses. All cooking is done on an open fire or kerosene stove.

Sanitation and hygiene are generally poor. Most settlements use pit latrines, although bush areas around settlements are often used for toilet purposes instead.

Settlement water supply.

Summary

Rural-urban drift occurs in most developing countries in the world.

Rural-urban drift started in Papua New Guinea in the 1950s and caused a rapid growth in the population of Port Moresby.

People are **pushed** from the rural areas by:

- overpopulation
- loss of food gardens
- tribal conflict.

People are **pulled** to the urban areas by:

- employment opportunities
- better health and education services
- the 'bright lights' of the city.

Migrants have no resources when they first come to the city and many remain unemployed.

Migrants build shelters from scrap materials on any unused land they find.

Most migrants earn a living using their own skills.

Sharing is important in urban settlements to help people without work to survive.

Religion is important to urban migrants all over the world as well as in Papua New Guinea.

Sanitation standards are generally low in urban settlements.

The National Capital District Interim Commission (NCDIC) is helping to upgrade the standard of living for urban settlers.

Activities

Exercises

1. Fill in the blanks in the following passage.

   Rural people in many __________ countries leave the countryside and move to the large cities hoping for a better life. This is known as __________-__________ __________. Factors which cause people to move away from their home areas are called __________ factors. __________ factors attract people to the cities. People who move to the cities are known as __________. They often have no work and build houses out of __________ __________ on __________ land.

2. Copy out and complete the following table to show a number of factors that cause people to move from rural to urban areas.

PUSH FACTORS	PULL FACTORS

3. Draw a column graph to show the growth of the population of Port Moresby since 1947. Use the figures in the table on page 43.

Things to discuss

1. Are there any groups of settlers in your province? Discuss the reasons why people may have come there to settle.
2. Do people move into or out of your area? Discuss the reasons why people move. What advantages do the migrants want to obtain?
3. Does life in Port Moresby attract you? With a group of students from your class discuss the reasons why you feel this way.

Things to do

1. Organise a debate in your school between all the grade 8 classes. The topic should be:
   'Life in the village is better than life in the city'.
2. Make a list of all the things people living in settlements have to spend money on, and try to find out how much each costs per fortnight.
3. Make a list of all the activities you think settlers can do to earn money. How much work is done compared to the amount of money earned?

8. Urban Communities: Cities

A city is a very large urban centre. A city has many people living in it and has buildings for many different purposes.

Cities can be divided into areas according to the purposes of the buildings in those areas. The word zone is usually used instead of area. The diagram shows the land use zones of a typical city. Shops, offices and banks (commercial buildings) are usually found in the centre of the city. This is called the **Central Business District.** The administrative centre is often located here as well. In a ring around the commercial zone, factories (**light industry**) and older residential houses are found. Most people live in the **residential zone** situated towards the edges of the city. Mixed up among these different zones are open spaces, parks and playing fields, for people's **recreation**.

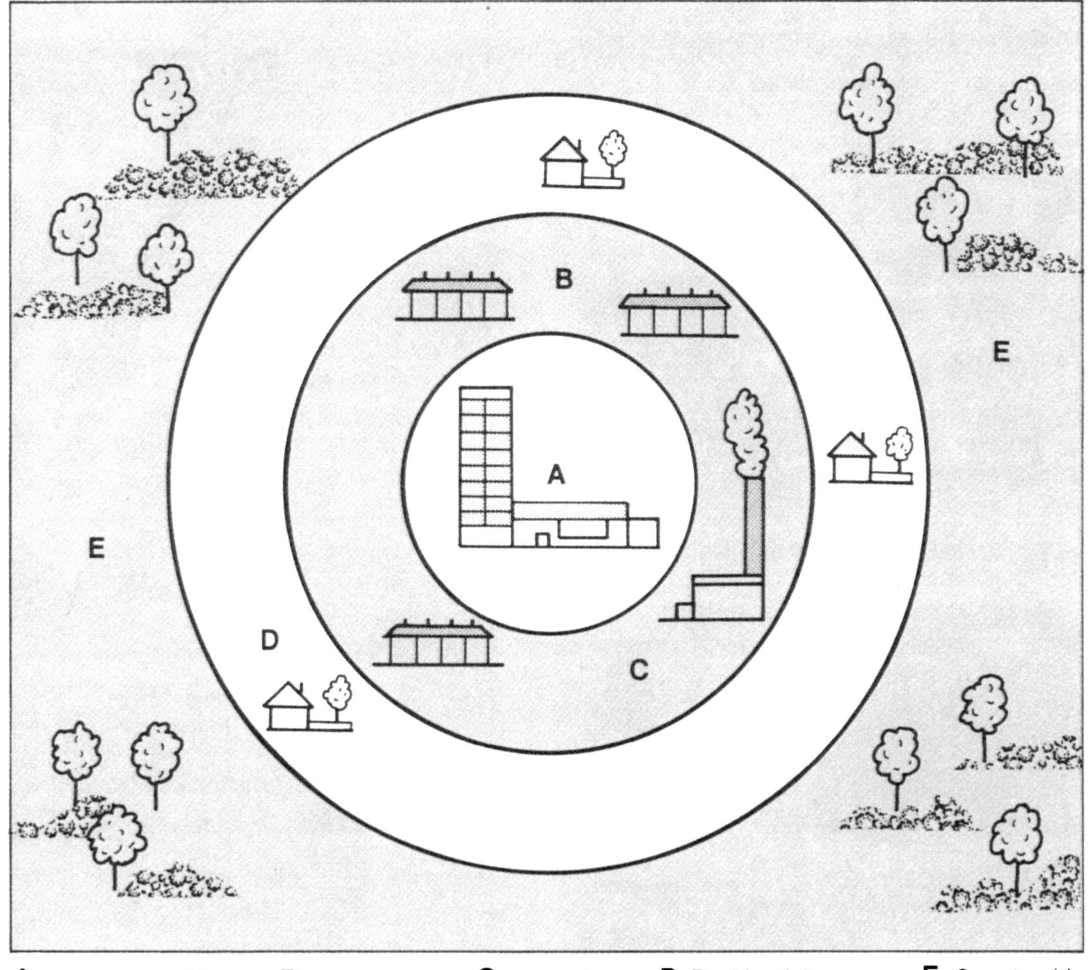

A Shops and offices **B** Old houses **C** Factories **D** Residential zones **E** Countryside

Land-use zones of a typical city.

Port Moresby

Port Moresby, like other cities in the world, can be divided into areas depending on the activities in those areas. These areas are called **land-use zones**.

Hanuabada — an urban village.

Luxury residences on Touaguba Hill.

Tall buildings in downtown Port Moresby.

Gerehu Residential Estate.

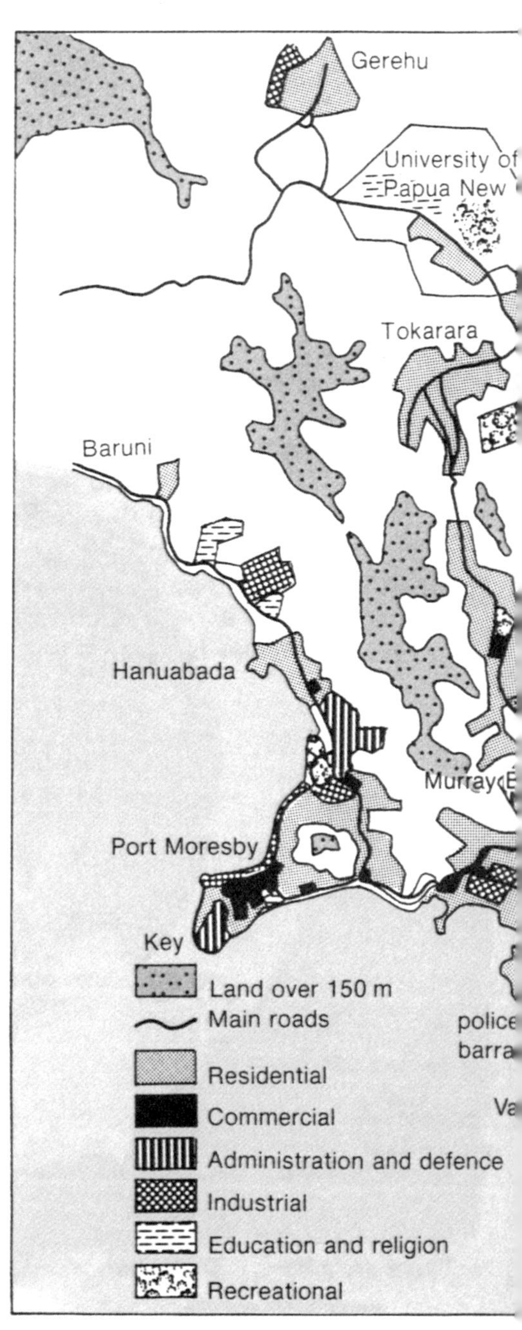

ni City Centre.

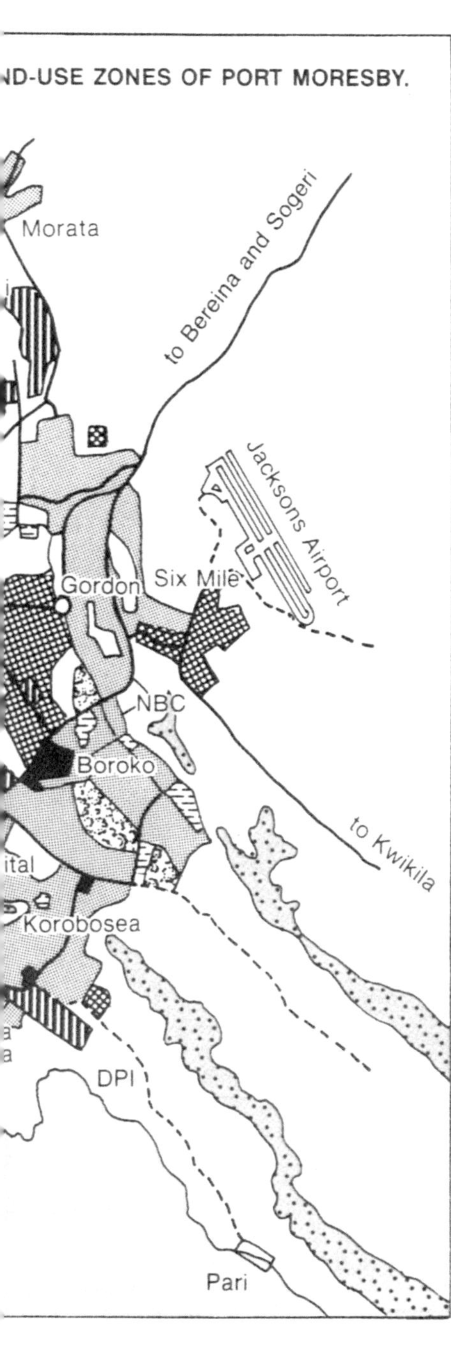

Gordon Industrial Estate.

Garden City Shopping Centre.

Sir Hubert Murray Stadium.

You will notice from the map on pages 50–1, that the pattern of land-use zones in Port Moresby is not as simple as the one shown in the diagram. There are several reasons for this:

- the lack of spare land for new buildings on the original downtown Port Moresby site
- the shape of the land. There are many steep hills in Port Moresby that are difficult to build on.
- the very rapid growth of Port Moresby since the 1950s.

Land-use zones of Port Moresby

The map on pages 50–1 shows the main land-use zones in Port Moresby in 1987. The photographs show examples of buildings in each zone and the activities that go on there.

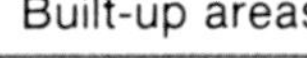

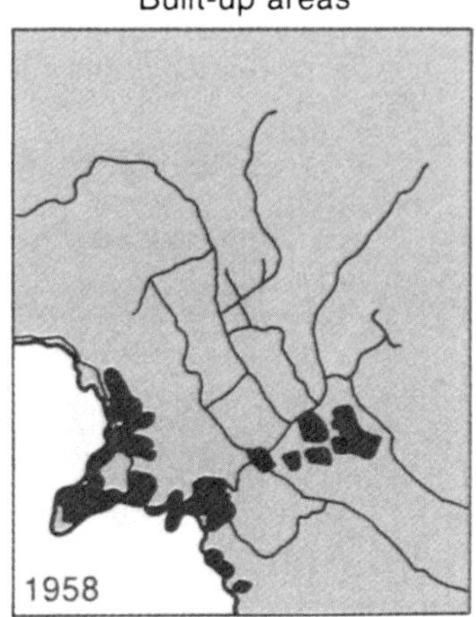

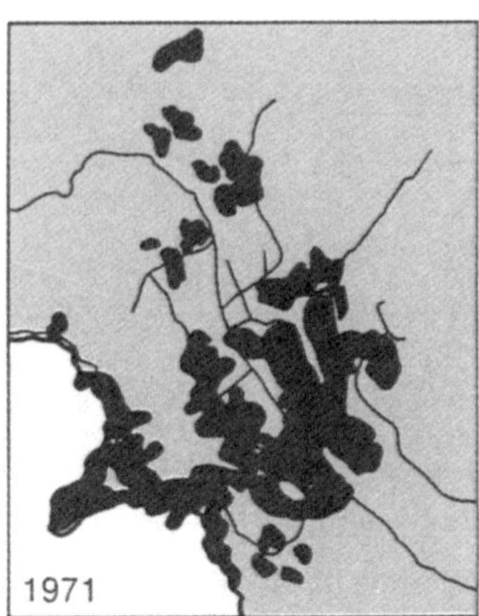

Town boundaries

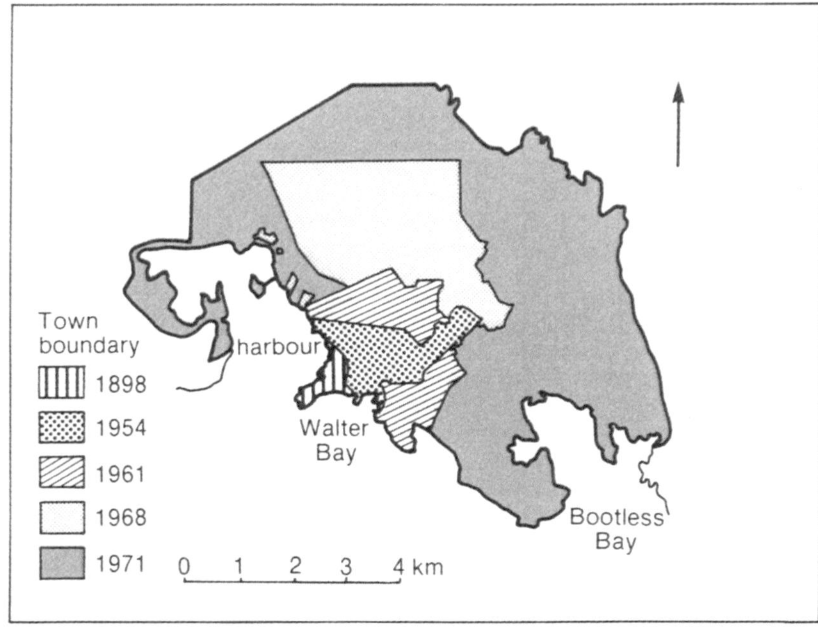

Growth of Port Moresby, 1942-71.

Living in Port Moresby

Employment

People come from all over Papua New Guinea to work in Port Moresby. The table below shows the number of people engaged in money-earning activities in Port Moresby in 1980.

ACTIVITY	NUMBER
Working for wages	34 500
Running a business	1 000
Farming/fishing for money	500
Total	36 000

The total population of Port Moresby in 1980 was 122 000. This means that only about 30 per cent of the people were employed. Of course many of the people not employed were students, children or housewives. There are, however, many people in Port Moresby who do not have jobs but who would like to work.

Hugos apartment block.

Housing

There are many different types of residential houses in Port Moresby. Foreign diplomats and rich businessmen occupy the luxury housing in downtown Port Moresby. Boroko, Korobosea and Gordon residential areas have houses that were mainly built in the 1960s and 70s. Many government workers rent these houses.

Self-help housing in Hohola.

The new housing areas at Tokarara and Gerehu began as a response to the increasing population. Morata and Hohola have expanded because people have bought land there and built their own houses.

High Covenant houses in Korobosea.

There is a general housing shortage in Port Moresby and many houses are overcrowded. In downtown Port Moresby, developers are building tall blocks of flats. This means that more people can live on the same area of land.

Families

There are many pressures on families living in the city. The traditional ways of sharing and working together in extended groups do not work well. Problems occur when wantoks come to stay. Often they do not want to return to the village. Often they have no work and cannot contribute to the living costs.

Everything in the city costs money. When too many people try to live off one wage, hardship occurs. This often leads to conflicts within the family. Because of these pressures the traditional type of community does not exist in the city. People meet and interact in ways different from those in traditional communities. Many city residents live as nuclear families—mother, father and children only—because that is all they can afford to do.

Community activities

There are many activities for the people in Port Moresby to take part in. These include clubs, sports, church meetings, cinemas, night clubs and discos. Various provincial groups hold regular meetings and organise activities together. People also meet to share ideas about their favourite hobbies or pastimes. These include clubs for bush-walking, model aeroplanes, shell collecting, choral singing, and even computer enthusiasts.

Services

People cannot satisfy their own needs in the city. The NCDIC provides

Drive-in cinema.

Cooking outside.

services such as water, sewage and garbage disposal. Electricity is supplied by the Electricity Commission. However, all residents have to pay for these services. People who do not pay their bills have these services cut off. Some households in the city cook outside on a wood fire and use candles for lighting because they cannot afford electricity.

Education and health services are of a high standard. However they cannot keep up with the rapidly growing population. Each year, many children cannot get into community schools. Nurses have to work many hours of overtime to care for their patients.

Transport services are provided by public motor vehicles and taxis. The PMVs are particularly busy between 7.00 a.m. to 8.00 a.m. and 4.00 p.m. to 6.00 p.m. on weekdays. This is the time that most people travel to and from work and so is called the **rush hour**.

Tokarara water tank.

Problems

Although many people come to Port Moresby looking for a better life, many of them meet problems they do not encounter in the rural areas.

Lack of housing is one problem already mentioned. This results in overcrowding and often leads to family conflict.

Unemployment is a big problem and is increasing each year. Unemployment has been blamed for a rise in crime in Port Moresby. Many criminals are school dropouts who cannot find work after they leave school.

The high cost of living causes hardship to many people in Port Moresby. In 1987 bills for services could total over K50 and food over K100 per fortnight. On top of this there are school fees, health bills and clothing costs. Many people have to do without the luxuries they thought they would have when they first came to Port Moresby.

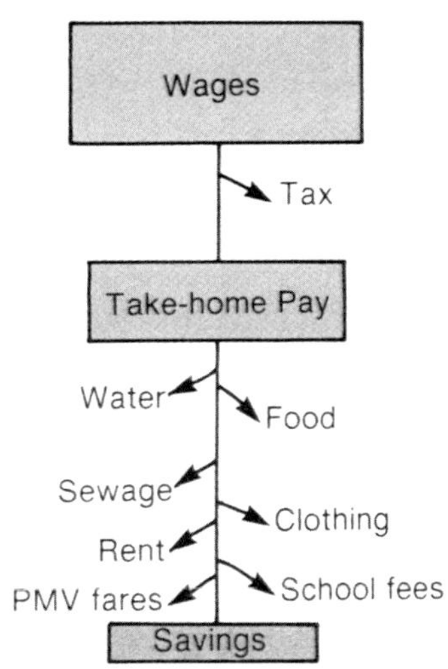

The high cost of living.

Pollution and traffic jams are serious problems in many cities in the world because of population increases. Exhaust fumes from diesel engines and smoke from burning hillsides are already causing air pollution in Port Moresby. Pollution from motor vehicles will increase as the population increases. This will soon become a serious problem in Port Moresby as well.

A youth being arrested.

Diesel fumes from a PMV.

Summary

Port Moresby can be divided into land-use zones according to the way the land is used:

- commercial — the main shopping and business zones. Boroko and downtown Port Moresby are the two main centres.
- residential — where people live
- industrial — where most factories are found. Gordon has a large area of light industry
- recreational — scattered all over the city
- educational and religious.

Lack of land near the coast and rapid population growth has caused Port Moresby to expand inland.

Only 30 per cent of the people in Port Moresby work for wages.

Port Moresby has a shortage of housing, resulting in overcrowding of many households.

Nuclear families are more common than extended families in Port Moresby because of the high cost of living.

Port Moresby has many different activities where people from all over the city meet to share their ideas.

Essential services are provided to all households, but they must be paid for. This adds to the high cost of living.

There are many problems for people living in Port Moresby that they do not encounter in rural areas. These problems are:

- lack of housing, leading to overcrowding
- unemployment, blamed for the increase in urban crime
- high cost of living
- traffic congestion, causing overcrowding of the roads
- pollution.

Activities

Exercises

1. Fill in the blanks in the following sentences.

   (a) A city is a very large __________ centre with many buildings for __________ purposes.

   (b) Cities can be divided into ____ - ____ __________ according to the purposes of the buildings there.

   (c) Buildings for commercial purposes, such as banks and shops, are usually found in the __________ of the city. This is often called the __________ __________ __________.

   (d) Factories and small industries are usually located in a ring around the commercial centre or following main transport routes out of the city. This is called the __________ zone.

   (e) Most people live in the __________ zone which is often located on the __________ of the city.

   (f) Playing fields, parks and open spaces are usually scattered around the city for __________ purposes.

2. Study the land-use map of Port Moresby.

   (a) Copy the following table into your exercise book and complete by writing down the type of land use for each place listed. Look at the photographs in this chapter to help you decide.

PLACE	LAND USE
Downtown Port Moresby	Central Business District
Sir Hubert Murray Stadium	
Hornibrook's Engineering	
Garden City Mall	
Touagouba Hill	
Waigani	
Gerehu Estate	
Bank of Papua New Guinea	
Hanuabada	
Murray Barracks	
Boroko	
University of Papua New Guinea	

   (b) Write a paragraph to describe why the development of Port Moresby is different from the general model shown on page 49.

Things to discuss

1. Discuss the effects of living in Port Moresby on traditional family links in Papua New Guinea. Are these effects good or bad?
2. Discuss and compare the way of life of people in a rural community with the way people live in the city. Act out a short play to show some of these differences.

Things to do

1. Collect newspaper photographs that show how people live in both rural and urban areas. Make a poster to show differences and similarities between the two ways of life.
2. **(a)** Make a list of all the benefits and advantages gained by living in the city.
   (b) Make a list of all the problems that people living in the city may have.
   (c) Which is better, living in the city or living in the countryside? Write a paragraph to answer this question, giving reasons for your answer.
3. Draw a map of your local area to show the land use of different areas and the services that are available. Make sure that you include a key and a scale.
4. Study the following list of the world's 20 largest cities.
   (a) On an outline map of the world, mark in and label the location of these cities and the name of the country they are in.
   (b) How many of these cities are in developing countries?
   (c) Which are the fastest-growing cities? In which part of the world are they located?
   (d) How many of these cities are likely to have problems caused by rural-urban drift?

CITY	POPULATION (millions)	CENSUS YEAR	1990 estimate (millions)
New York	16.1	1980	15.3
Mexico City	14.8	1979	21.3
Tokyo	11.6	1981	17.2
Shanghai	11.4	1970	12.0
Buenos Aires	9.9	1980	11.7
Los Angeles	9.5	1980	10.5
Calcutta	9.1	1981	12.6
Paris	8.6	1985	9.0
Seoul	8.4	1980	11.5
Moscow	8.3	1982	9.2
Bombay	8.2	1981	11.9
Chicago	7.9	1980	not available
Beijing	7.6	1970	9.5
Sao Paulo	7.1	1980	18.8
London	6.7	1981	9.5
Jakarta	6.5	1980	9.3
Delhi	5.7	1981	9.2
Philadelphia	5.5	1980	not available
Cairo	5.1	1976	10.0
Rio de Janeiro	5.1	1981	11.4

Note: These figures are from the latest official census of each country. 1987 estimates put most of the populations much higher.

Glossary

WORD	PAGE	MEANING
artisans	24	Skilled craftsmen, e.g. carpenters.
cash income	13	Money earned.
castes	24	Groups in India that have different status.
Central Business District	49	The part of a city where most of the commercial and business activities take place.
community	14	All the people who live in a particular place.
co-operation	32	Working together.
conserve	12	To use a resource carefully and not all at once.
cost of living	56	How much you must pay to live properly.
democratic	5	Everyone has a vote in the way things are done.
dry savanna	16	Grassland with scattered trees.
emergency services	33	Services that help other people when sudden trouble happens.
employment	40	Having a paid job.
irrigation	22	A water supply system for crops.
land-use zones	50	Areas where the land is mainly used for one purpose, e.g. residential.
light industry	49	Small manufacturing places, e.g. furniture workshops.
migration	39	Moving from one place to another.
nomadic herders	18	People who wander from place to place looking after herds of animals.
an organisation	8	A group of people that has a particular aim or purpose.
padi	22	A rice field.
prevailing wind	16	The wind that is blowing most of the time.
recreation	49	Relaxation, play.
religion	2	Belief in a god or gods.
residential zone	49	An area of a city where people have their houses.
sanitation	47	Keeping a place clean and healthy.
specialisation	25	People doing one particular task.
unemployment	55	Having no paid work.

Index